Pre-Public₂

"Informative, well researched and entertaining... with a clear roadmap for increased profit and customer satisfaction excellence." *Bill Emerson, Vice Chairman, Quicken Loans Inc.*

"Jim Deitch has written a must-read primer for anyone serious about understanding this industry, especially in the wake of the changes in recent years." *Dave Stevens, President & CEO, Mortgage Bankers Association of America*

"... Jim Deitch did a great job breaking down the industry threats and filling in the holes." *David Motley, President, Colonial Savings*

"A powerful read on the industry that will surely inform mortgage professionals on how to embrace technology and change company culture, all with a view to achieving customer satisfaction." *Jonathan Corr, President & CEO, Ellie Mae, Inc.*

"The book is written from the eyes of an industry CEO, for industry CEOs and their teams." *Deb Still, President & CEO, Pulte Mortgage LLC*

"Jim did a great job of gathering information across a broad array of executives. He's woven this into a comprehensive chart of history and current reflections about where we've been and where we are as an industry." *Stan Middleman, CEO, Freedom Mortgage*

"Jim builds a conceptual model to digest the rapid advance of technology and how to apply it as a "C" level executive. A clear road map to customer satisfaction excellence and outstanding profitability." *Susan Stewart, President & CEO, SWBC Mortgage Corporation*

"Jim Deitch takes you inside the back offices, strategy and industry leaders perspective of the top mortgage banking firms in America. A must read for the industry and consumers." *Bill Cosgrove, President & CEO, Union Home Mortgage Corp.*

"Jim picked 25 'maverick CEOs' for interviews. These mavericks collectively have a great vision for the future of Mortgage Banking and the transformation necessary in the lending business model. Very valuable insights." *Cody Pearce, President & Co-founder, Cascade Financial Services, LLC*

"This book addresses the exact concerns a CEO in the mortgage industry faces. It does so in clear and concise way." *Jim MacLeod, Executive Chairman, CoastalStates Bank*

"Jim Deitch takes readers through the challenges that customers and lenders are facing in the Mortgage Banking Industry." *Patrick Sinks, CEO & Director, MGIC Investment Corp.*

"Success in today's mortgage industry depends on the combination of intelligent process and advanced technology. A must-read for executives seeking to understand the future of mortgage banking." *Jerry Schiano, President & CEO, New Penn Financial, LLC*

Simple yet informative, and conceptual yet practical, Digitally Transforming the Mortgage Banking Industry is a book designed to help a lender achieve best in class profits and customer satisfaction." *Phil DeFronzo, CEO & Co-founder, Norcom Mortgage*

"Jim Deitch has written a good overview of the mortgage industry today. Drawing upon insights from leaders, mortgage industry data and examples from other industries, Jim's book sheds considerable light on the post-financial crisis mortgage industry." *Rich Bennion, Executive Vice President, HomeStreet Bank*

"A comprehensive survey of industry thought leaders presented in a clear and concise manner." *Steve Shank, President & CEO, Flinchbaugh Engineering, Inc.*

"The book provides in-depth knowledge from industry thought leaders. It balances technology and process very appropriately." *Tim Nguyen, President & Co-founder, BeSmartee*

"Detailed, Powerful, and Concise. Read it and share it with your executives. Jim describes the future landscape of lending, and how to prosper in the coming Digital Mortgage revolution." *Nathan Burch, CEO, Vellum Mortgage, LLC*

"The book uses powerful examples from the industry thought leaders on transforming the mortgage banking business to a high profit, high customer satisfaction model." *Kevin Pearson, President, CalAtlantic Mortgage*

"If you're a leader in the mortgage industry or aspire to be one, this is a must read. Jim combines the expertise of current leaders with compelling data to help drive a successful approach in today's - and tomorrow's - mortgage market which is poised for disruptive efficiency improvement and to be well aligned with changing applicant demographics." *Barrett Burns, President & CEO, VantageScore Solutions*

"An interaction with Jim on the mortgage industry is always an education. This book is no different, managing to take the thoughts and information garnered from the interviews and painting a clear picture that Mortgage executives can easily interpret and apply to their business and see actual results from it." *Martin Kerr, President, Bestborn Business Solutions*

DIGITALLY TRANSFORMING

the

MORTGAGE BANKING INDUSTRY

THE MAVERICK'S QUEST
for Outstanding Profit <u>and</u> Customer Satisfaction

James M. Deitch CPA, CMB

Digitally Transforming the Mortgage Banking Industry

Copyright © 2018 James M. Deitch CPA, CMB

ISBN-13: 978-1-9856-6817-1

Disclaimer: This book contains the author's opinions resulting from discussions with other executives, experiences from 30 years in the mortgage banking industry and research. The author may have had prior, ongoing or planned business relationships with any or all executives or companies identified in this book, and readers should assume the author is not independent with respect to any product, service, executive or company identified within this book. The quotes from executives in this book are used by the author with their permission and the executive quotes may not be reprinted or redistributed without the express permission of the executive. None of the executive quotes in this book should be considered as an endorsement of the author's opinions in this book, which are the result of discussions with executives with a variety of views. The information provided in this book is intended to be used solely as a basis for the reader's discussion with the reader's executive team and professional advisors and not as a substitute for legal or other professional advice. The author and publisher expressly disclaim any responsibility for the results of the reader's use of the material in this book.

Dedication

———

The MBA Opens Doors Foundation is a non-profit organization dedicated to aiding families with a critically ill or injured child by making their mortgage or rent payment. MBA Opens Doors currently works directly with nine children's hospitals to identify families in need.

Opens Doors holds a special place in my heart. All royalties from this book will be donated to the Opens Doors Foundation.

Acknowledgements

Thank you to Judy, my wife, for encouragement, assistance, and practical advice, and most of all for being a role model and mother to our kids.

To my children Michael and Christina, and grandchildren Marie, Belle, Colin and Caroline for your constant inspiration.

To Alex Henderson, my friend, business partner, and consigliere for thirty years, who more or less kept me out of foolish adventures and helped greatly in the concept and structure of the book. To Don Bishop, as well, for 45 years of friendship, business, and fun, and for being a fellow entrepreneur.

To Rob Peterson and Maylin Casanueva for your strategic knowledge and perspective on mortgage banking and capital markets and helping our business partners in so many ways.

To the mavericks: Barrett Burns, Bill Cosgrove, Bill Emerson, Byron Boston, Cody Pearce, Dave Motley, Dave Stevens, Deb Still, Ed Robinson, Jamie Korus-Pearce, Jerry Rader, Jerry Schiano, Jim MacLeod, Jonathan Corr, Julie Piepho, Kevin Pearson, Martin Kerr, Nathan

Burch, Nima Ghamsari, Patty Arvielo, Rick Arvielo, Patrick Sinks, Phil DeFronzo, Rich Bennion, Stan Middleman, Steve Shank, Susan Stewart, and Tim Nguyen. Thank you so very much for your willingness to share your thought leadership. Without your thought leadership, this book would not be possible.

To Eleni Valasis for your outstanding writing, editing, and research work. You have great gifts.

To Anthony Nguyen for technical research, analytics, and help with production of the manuscript. Dennis Kluck, Brett Hamsher, and Pam Mennie for analytics and research assistance. To Liz French and Mauricio Valverde for administrative support. Thank you to Barb Wise for all your design and graphic work over the years.

To Teraverde®'s partners, customers, and friends – you make this all possible!

Table of Contents

Introduction

What is a "maverick"? He or she can best be described as a groundbreaker, a pioneer. A maverick takes calculated risks to grow, to invoke change. In many ways, a maverick is an initiator, someone willing to explore unfamiliar territory and try on innovative ideas when and where others are not.

The world of mortgage banking has been tied down by traditional ways of doing things. In fact, there are protocols in place that trace back multiple decades to just after the Great Depression. While industries around us have been exploring new ways of doing things and (perhaps most importantly) new technologies, mortgage banking has tended to stay with the tried and true.

While some in the mortgage industry maintain an "if it ain't broke, don't fix it" mentality, more and more maverick thought leaders are turning to transformation, be it via process, technology, or product innovation.

And it cannot come soon enough.

Since the Great Recession of 2008-2010, the U.S. has experienced significant economic shifts, but also seismic cultural shifts. While middle class ambitions in the past centered on the split-level home, today's homebuyer is turning more and more to less traditional housing options. What's more, the contemporary homebuyer does not necessarily fit the traditional mold defined by both the industry and regulation.

What can the mortgage industry do to respond to these changes? What are the discussions taking place amongst thought leaders to drive these changes?

The origin of this book began when my daughter, Christina, was in the process of purchasing a home in the Frisco, Texas area. I recommended a reputable lender to her. About halfway through the process she called and said "Dad, your industry is really screwed up. I applied for a credit card and was approved in a few minutes. I applied for a loan for a car and within a few minutes, signed the paperwork and drove out with a brand-new vehicle. I applied for a mortgage and I keep getting asked question after question after question and the process never seems to end. I don't know where I am in the process and my loan officer can't really tell me what's coming next. I can't believe that all the smart people in the mortgage banking industry can't make this a simple process for consumers without all this nonsense."

She and her husband did eventually close on the mortgage loan. What's interesting is that both she and her husband are engineers, so process and efficiency are not exactly alien to them. What's more, Christina's specialty at the time was lean manufacturing for a major defense contractor. From her perspective, mortgage banking was highly inefficient, confused, *and* confusing.

I asked her specifically what was wrong with the process. She felt the mortgage process was poorly defined, poorly executed, and very inefficient.

Lean manufacturing has a very specific process that is followed closely, with little or no wasted time. All required materials to complete a process are on hand when needed. Complex electronic and mechanical products are manufactured in quantity, economically, and with zero defects.

As a contrast, during the mortgage process, she was asked for the same bank statements on three different occasions and asked for additional paystubs and tax documents after being assured that all the documents needed had been supplied. Not to mention that she felt poorly informed during the process, and very frustrated. She was especially irked because she and her husband were well qualified for the loan they applied for. She repeatedly said, "Dad, I financed a new car through the dealer's finance department with no money down and drove the car away from start to finish in about 30 minutes. The mortgage process took 60 days, had a large down payment and the *house can't be driven away.*"

My daughter is not the only one asking questions about the 'what' and the 'why' in mortgage banking today. The catalyst that made me realize these ideas should go into a book came when I served as a panelist for "FinTech and the Future" discussion at the 2017 Mortgage Bankers Association ("MBA ") Chairman's Conference. The MBA publishes reports setting out aggregated data for several hundred lenders. I observed that the MBA peer data for the first quarter of 2017 showed the average cost of operational labor was about $2,600. In 2017, General Motors used $2,350 of operational direct labor to manufacture a typical vehicle. How could it take more operational labor to manufacture a stack of paper than it takes to make a new car?

The panelists discussed that the average cost of a loan was $8,800, with an average balance of about $240,000 and an interest rate just under 4% at the time. The $8,800 cost of the mortgage loan was almost 4% of the principal balance. If the average cost was reduced to $5,000 (about the cost in 2010), the $3,800 cost reduction would equate to about 3/8% interest rate reduction to the consumer. That's real money! Many attendees approached me after the presentation and asked questions, and we spoke about MBA averages versus the best performers in the industry. Several asked about the paltry profitability level of about 10 basis points in the first quarter of 2017. One question really hit me: "How does a lender consistently earn 100 basis points or more in pretax income?" More on that question in a moment.

Jonathan Corr, a panelist and CEO of Ellie Mae commented, "Somebody should write a book on this." That seemed like a pretty good idea. But how to proceed?

The prior MBA Chairman's Conference had been held in Southeast Florida. At the time, my wife, Judy, commented how the temperature for the conference was just perfect. It was 76 degrees, which happens to be the average temperature for the year in Southeast Florida. It also happened to be the average temperature in Death Valley, CA. The difference was the Death Valley temperature ranged from a low of 37 degrees at night to a high of 115 degrees during the day. Statisticians define the temperature variance in Southeast Florida as a small 'standard deviation'[1], while describing Death Valley's

---

[1] Standard deviation is a number used to tell how measurements for a group are spread out from the average (mean) or expected value. A low standard deviation means that most of the numbers are very close to the average. A high standard

as a large 'standard deviation' in temperature, as illustrated in the graph below. In other words, the temperature average is the same in Southeast Florida as Death Valley, but *livability* differs significantly between the two regions, due to their respective standard deviations in temperature.

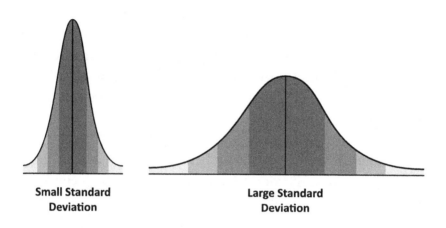

Small Standard Deviation   **Large Standard Deviation**

Could the same statistical phenomenon be true for mortgage banking processes, loan officer performance, cost to produce, and operational efficiency averages? Could the variance spread affect industry profitability as the Death Valley temperature variances affect livability? Meaning, could averages mask very good and very poor performance at the edges of both sides of the curve?

Turning to the Mavericks

I met with several of my senior team: Maylin Casanueva, Alex Henderson, and Rob Peterson to discuss these concepts. The group

deviation means that the numbers are spread out. (https://simple.wikipedia.org/wiki/Standard_deviation)

noted that there were significant differences in profitability, cost, and efficiency among lenders in general and among lenders in our client base. As research, we analyzed anonymized data for (among other statistics) turnaround time, loan officer productivity, operational costs, and profitability. I spoke with several CEOs and senior executives, and their suggestion was to look for CEOs who were making a significant difference for their companies and for the industry. The statistics suggested there were significant performance differences based on strategy and execution. Could one intentionally transform the mortgage banking process to systemically produce a high customer satisfaction, high profit, low cost model? If so, how?

Notice I didn't include the words, "best practice", when describing a high customer satisfaction, high profit, low cost, high employee retention model. The reason is that "best practice" can sometimes be viewed as a generic solution that should be applied to all lenders. In my discussions with CEOs, as well as in my observations of the industry, I've seen that lenders are as diverse as the people that run them. What may make sense as a "best practice" in a consumer direct lender may not apply to a traditional retail lender. That's why I describe the *results* of a lender's operation: high customer satisfaction, high profit, low cost, high employee retention model. That's more important than "best practice".

What's more, I've long known that CEOs focus on outputs or how to achieve desired results, not inputs like "best practices".

Thus, I decided to seek out transformative CEOs[2] who are ground-breakers and pioneers in the mortgage banking and related industries to uncover how the best become the best at high customer satisfaction, high profit, low cost, high employee retention metrics. For example, Quicken Loans has the highest customer satisfaction for seven years running according to J.D. Power, a nationally-known customer survey firm. How did Quicken do it?

A close advisor of mine, Don Bishop of Affinigent, focused our search on the concept of "maverick CEOs". As the people willing to explore new territory and try on new ideas when and where others are not, these mavericks would be uniquely qualified to guide this conversation. It turns out that the "mavericks" are producing top performance results, too. So, my first interview request went to Bill Emerson, CEO of Quicken, and a fellow panelist at the MBA Chairman's Conference. Bill kindly accepted, as did about 25 additional CEOs[3] who I consider mavericks in the industry, including fellow panelists Nima Ghamsari of Blend and Jonathan Corr of Ellie Mae.

At the outset, I envisioned this book as starting where a potential customer's search for a mortgage began, whether it was on the

[2] In the interest of full disclosure, having spent 30 years in the mortgage banking industry, I have had business and personal relationships, past and present, with virtually all of the executives interviewed in this book. The discussions with any executive or individual that occurred in writing this book should not be construed as an endorsement of any individual, product, service or company. As my counsel has suggested, "The author may have had prior, ongoing or planned business relationships with any or all executives or companies identified in this book, and readers should assume the author is not independent with respect to any product, service, executive or company identified within this book". While there are too few maverick CEOs, the 25 interviewed for this book are not alone in the industry.

[3] This book groups Chairman, Chief Executive Officer, and President titles under the collective term 'CEO' as shorthand for the executive responsible for mortgage banking strategy and overall execution.

Internet, referrals from friends, realtors etc. I'll call this "Initial Interest" of the consumer in a loan. The book would focus on the process through loan settlement, and then on to servicing. I was very fortunate to talk to CEOs who thought much more broadly about the mortgage banking industry than the process from consumer interest through servicing. The CEOs spoke about their company's culture, their passion for helping customers, customers' views of their needs for housing (both rental, traditional, and non-traditional housing) and the retention of customers for life. They also spoke of process, technology, efficiency, and innovation. Those discussions reframed the direction of this book to a much broader look at mortgage banking transformation.

A complete list of the Mavericks, their positions, and their companies at the time of their interview follows shortly. Judy Piepho of Cornerstone Lending spoke about the lifestyle needs of a person seeking shelter. These lifestyle needs included whether to rent or buy and what size of home would make the most individualized sense. Cody Pearce from Cascade spoke about extending the consumer need to affordable manufactured housing. Cody identified some of the possible misconceptions that some in our industry have regarding manufactured housing, but how manufactured housing can be one of the most interesting opportunities for affordable homeownership in the United States.

Bill Emerson of Quicken spoke of "no excuses" when working with customers. Rich Bennion of HomeStreet spoke about the difficulty that non-traditional borrowers face when trying to get a mortgage approved post Dodd-Frank. Dave Stevens of MBA spoke about the need to have competition when contemplating the future of the government-sponsored enterprises ("GSEs"), and to ensure that there is equal access to credit for consumers as well equal access to the GSE and mortgage investors for all sizes and shapes of Mortgage

Bankers. Barrett Burns of VantageScore recounted his efforts to expand the current credit scoring regimes to accommodate more borrowers who don't initially fit the current method of credit scoring, but who are both potentially scorable and underserved. Stan Middleman noted that not all potential borrowers are best served as homeowners if they cannot meet the costs of owning a home long-term.

Tim Nguyen of BeSmartee looked forward to a future in which a consumer can obtain a mortgage commitment and close as fast as a consumer purchasing a car can do today. Nima Ghamsari of Blend spoke about demystifying the consumer mortgage experience. Jonathan Corr of Ellie Mae spoke of the tendency of lenders to patch poor workflows with "human spackle", which doesn't remediate poor processes and often results in more "checkers checking the checkers". Jim MacLeod of CoastalStates reminded us of the formidable barriers that the current regulatory regime has of blocking innovation in the mortgage lending marketplace. Pat Sinks of MGIC spoke about innovation and how borrowers can use private mortgage insurance to obtain a loan with a smaller down payment. He also spoke about the concern of rising housing prices in certain areas in the country including California, which could be setting up another large price adjustment downward when a recession occurs. Ed Robinson of Fifth Third spoke about meeting a customer through a channel that serves the borrower exactly where and how they want to be served.

These were just a few of the many conversations I had with leaders such as Bill Cosgrove, Stan Middleman, Susan Stewart, Deb Still, Jerry Rader, Martin Kerr, Nathan Burch, Phil DeFronzo, Jamie Korus-Pearce, Byron Boston, and more. Given these conversations and feedback, the book now looks at how the industry serves the needs of both purchasers and renters of homes. It looks at the generational attributes of non-traditional borrowers. It looks at those innovating how mortgage loans are originated and how to substantially increase the profitability and efficiency of the mortgage banking process. Collectively, we'll outline an approach to a lender's journey to and through a Digitally Transformed Mortgage Banking platform.

Virtually all CEOs described the mortgage lending process as extremely complex, with capital markets, regulators, GSEs, and sheer inertia contributing to this complexity. Below is a chart[4] mapping the movement of data to various users throughout the mortgage process. It's condensed from a much larger format, but you'll get the idea. This is not an easy business to master.

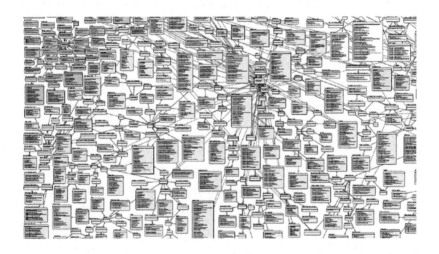

So, how does one turn the convoluted process above into a method that generates 100 basis points or more consistently? Let's turn to the mavericks.

---

[4] Presentation by Mike Fratantoni, Ph.D., Chief Economist & Senior Vice President, Mortgage Bankers Association of America, January 2017, Independent Mortgage Bankers' conference.

Mavericks: The List

I'd like to introduce the mavericks who agreed to generously contribute their thought leadership to this book. They're alphabetically listed by first name:

CONTACT	TITLE	COMPANY
Barrett Burns	President & CEO	VantageScore Solutions, LLC
Bill Cosgrove	President & CEO	Union Home Mortgage Corp.
Bill Emerson	Vice Chairman	Quicken Loans Inc.
Byron Boston	President, CEO & Co-CIO	Dynex Capital Inc.
Cody Pearce	President & Co-Founder	Cascade Financial Services, LLC
David Motley	President	Colonial Savings
Dave Stevens	President & CEO	Mortgage Bankers Association of America
Deb Still	President & CEO	Pulte Mortgage LLC
Ed Robinson	Senior VP, Head of Mortgage	Fifth Third Mortgage
Jamie Korus-Pearce	President	Alliance Financial Resources LLC
Jerry Rader	President	Corridor Mortgage Group, Inc.
Jerry Schiano	President & CEO	New Penn Financial & Spring EQ
Jim MacLeod	Executive Chairman	CoastalStates Bank
Jonathan Corr	President & CEO	Ellie Mae, Inc.
Julie Piepho	President, National Operations	Cornerstone Home Lending, Inc.
Kevin Pearson	President	CalAtlantic Mortgage
Martin Kerr	CEO & Co-Founder	Bestborn Business Solution
Nathan Burch	President & COO	Vellum Mortgage, LLC
Nima Ghamsari	CEO & Co-Founder	Blend
Patty Arvielo	President & Co-Founder	New American Funding
Patrick Sinks	CEO & Director	MGIC Investment Corporation
Phil DeFronzo	CEO & Founder	Norcom Mortgage
Stan Middleman	CEO & Founder	Freedom Mortgage
Rich Bennion	EVP, Residential Construction & Affiliated Businesses	HomeStreet Bank Inc.
Steve Shank	President & CEO	Flinchbaugh Engineering, Inc.
Susan Stewart	President & CEO	SWBC Mortgage Corporation
Tim Nguyen	CEO & Co-Founder	BeSmartee

We'll cover the thoughts, actions, and initiatives that these transformational mavericks leverage in mortgage lending to challenge conventional wisdom. For those of you looking for a quicker summary of the thoughts gathered herein, I've also included a Summary section at the end of the book, which looks at many of the high-level ideas developed in depth throughout the work.

This journey has been enlightening for me. I hope it is for you, as well. Let's get started.

About the Author

James M. Deitch founded Teraverde® seven years ago, after serving as President and CEO of five federally chartered banks for over twenty-five years. Teraverde® now advises over 150 clients in mortgage banking, capital markets and financial technology, ranging from some of the largest U.S. financial institutions to independent mortgage bankers to community banks. Jim founded two national banks, including a top 50 national mortgage lender.

Jim holds a Master of Business Administration, with concentrations in Finance and Marketing, and a Bachelor of Science degree in accounting from Lehigh University. He is a Certified Mortgage Banker and, until he realized mortgage banking was a lot more interesting than public accounting, practiced as a CPA. Jim has been a director of both publicly traded and privately-owned banks and lenders through some very interesting times.

Jim's experience in residential mortgage banking for the last three decades on a retail, wholesale and correspondent basis led to an intense desire to learn about how technology could be applied to financial institutions. His experience includes multi-channel loan origination and sales management, mortgage product design, credit policy, hedging, securitization and loan servicing, and his beginning to end experience – and his love of high performance aircraft —has fueled his "need for speed" in applying technology to mortgage banking.

He has served on the Mortgage Bankers Association Residential Board of Governors and served as a CEO panelist and speaker for major financial institutions, financial industry associations, corporate clients, the Department of Defense and universities. Jim is a thought leader and has published numerous articles in the industry publications.

Jim lives in Naples, Florida.

CHAPTER ONE

The Transformative CEO – Vision, Culture and Customer Experience

I t's a different world out there today. While much of what grounds the mortgage industry was developed decades ago, the homebuyers who engage with the industry live in a very different world than the one that existed in the 1970s, 80s, or 90s.

What's different? The list is endless. From the way we earn to the way we envision life as a homeowner, many of the particulars that define "homebuyer" have changed drastically since the mid-twentieth century. We'll dial into all of this in greater detail in chapters to come, but suffice it to say issues such as wide diversity of income and employment, the size or nature of homes, and even the predictors of loan performance that we use are so far from where we were "back in the day" that it boggles the mind that the industry itself has changed very little.

What I heard again and again in my conversations with maverick CEOs is that they are embracing change and taking a transformative approach to the future of mortgage banking. In other words, many central figures in the industry are turning their minds to a new tomorrow and how they can Digitally Transform the Mortgage Banking Industry and their companies. What perhaps has not occurred yet is a cohesive vision, a strategic plan that can provide some clarity and serve as a guideline for the future of mortgage banking.

While it's perhaps overly ambitious to envision this book as creating that plan, my core ambition is that it can start at least a conversation around these ideas, and that we can come together as an industry to discuss a digitally transformative approach to mortgage banking that reacts to and works in tandem with the realities of a new world.

While most of the focus of this book looks to the future, it is important to remember how we got to the mortgage marketplace we have today. Stan Middleman, CEO of Freedom Mortgage said, "Some people in our business were bad historians." Meaning many in the industry did not consider the possibility of the length and depth of the Financial Crisis of 2007-2010.

The Financial Crisis became clear to virtually everyone in the western world in the summer of 2008. At that time, events created extreme financial stress and extreme lack of liquidity in the financial markets: the conservatorship of Freddie Mac and Fannie Mae; the failure of several large banks engaged in mortgage lending; the failure of major participants in the credit markets, including Lehman and AIG; and the unexpected actions and intervention of the federal government agencies in the financial markets as described herein. These multiple, unexpected and unprecedented events resulted in unusually large and rapid increases in unemployment and loan delinquency rates, reduction in housing values, losses in equity and credit markets, and unexpected changes in borrower behaviors through 'strategic defaults'.

Stan Middleman recounted how Freedom's strategy had to change quickly as the Financial Crisis unfolded. As an independent mortgage banker ("IMB"), liquidity was essential for continued operations; liquidity was shrinking in 2007 and virtually evaporated by late summer 2008 after Freddie Mac and Fannie Mae were placed into conservatorship. Freedom move quickly to focus on FHA and VA lending because liquidity in those products was assured.

> *When you are a small company, you have small issues. Big companies, big issues. [During 2007 and 2008, large companies] needed a lot of liquidity to get by. It was a real problem. So [for Freedom] it was really a liquidity issue at the end of the day. We took a route that created the safest loans possible. We were 90 percent GSE going into 2007. By 2008, we were 90 percent Ginnie Mae. Ginnie Mae provided liquidity by statute. Statutory liquidity is far different than discretionary liquidity. [By the end of 2008], we were in a pretty good place because we made that strategic change to focus to Ginnie Mae lending. Now later we paid a price for that decision, but given the price that we've paid I'd make that choice 10 times out of 10 times. Ginnie Mae couldn't put loans back at their discretion the way the GSEs could. And, in my experience from previous downturns and cycle issues, I knew that the GSEs would put loans back. I knew the market was overheated. And I knew there would be a correction. So, none of that was a big surprise to me.*

Mr. Middleman's strategic thinking and his business transformation strategy positioned Freedom for growth at a time when many other large independent mortgage bankers failed.

Deb Still served as an officer and ultimately Chairman of the Mortgage Bankers Association during some of the darkest days of the crisis. Her vision for the industry (while still running Pulte Mortgage) was well researched and clear. Pulte and many other mortgage bankers did not dive into subprime mortgage lending, but nonetheless all mortgage bankers were the "bad guys". As an observation, during a trip to Capitol Hill[5], Steve O'Connor on the MBA staff recounts a story where he ran into lobbyists from the tobacco industry. The tobacco lobbyists' comments were biting, to say the least, and ran along the lines of, "Glad to see the mortgage bankers on the Hill. Congress now hates you more than they hate us. Keep on coming up."

During the 2009-2010 period, according to MBA executives and staff, studies on consumer sentiment regarding the financial crisis put the blame on mortgage bankers and bankers in general. Capitol Hill denizens knew this and instinctively painted the industry participants with a broad brush. Many leaders would shrink back from plain talk. Deb spoke during a meeting with the Residential Board of Governors of the MBA about the path forward: take accountability, acknowledge the reputational damage, make it right for consumers, and move forward. Deb's discussions in a friendly audience were candid and straightforward as she shared the MBA's research.

---

[5] I served on the MBA Residential Board of Governors for 3 terms and represented the MBA as an industry executive on numerous occasions in meetings with legislators, regulators and administration staff during the period 2004-2010.

She was equally candid on Capitol Hill when testifying or meeting with legislators representing MBA as a member of the Association's industry leadership, as were her predecessors and successor Chairmen of the MBA[6] (each Chair serves a one-year term). The candid approach of the MBA executives and staff began to restore credibility with legislators, regulators, and borrowers. Deb (and her fellow MBA Chairmen) had a clear vision of the destination: a restoration of credibility, and they fashioned their message and plan accordingly.

Appendix 2 of this book is a more detailed visit through the Financial Crisis. Even for someone who lived through the events of late-summer 2008 to early 2009 as a financial institution CEO, the extraordinary tempo of deteriorating liquidity and market disruption is easy to forget. As Stan Middlemen points out, it's worth keeping this history in mind so we collectively don't become "bad historians" and forget how fast liquidity can vanish from the financial system.

The Vision and Culture Planning of the Maverick CEO

We've discussed the basics of being a maverick, but what does it mean to be a maverick leader in mortgage banking specifically? In my many conversations with everyone from Dave Stevens to Tim Nguyen, certain themes became clear. In fact, I began to see a pattern in the way these thought leaders were approaching their work, both on the micro and macro levels. Whether they were discussing in-house processes, or the industry writ large, certain patterns presented themselves again and again.

---

[6] Recent Prior Chairmen of the MBA include Rodrigo Lopez, CMB; Bill Emerson; Bill Cosgrove, CMB; E.J. Burke; Deb Still, CMB, Michael Young; and Michael Berman.

Without articulating it specifically, the strategy of each CEO contained healthy elements of the list below:

- The need to become the champion of a clear vision and culture, leading to a customer experience expectation of quality customer service and satisfaction for each channel served, whether it be consumer direct, retail[7], wholesale, correspondent or services partner;

- Including output metrics with regards to customer satisfaction, profitability, cost to produce, employee retention, defect-free loan files, and service levels in that vision;

- A compelling push to create processes and technology that innovate and lend in a way that meets customers' best interests, that best serve customer need, and that comply with the regulations that govern mortgage lending;

- A company culture that attracted and retained employee committed to the company vision and culture;

- A desire to challenge the "standard thinking" in the industry;

- A willingness to engage partners, competitors, legislators, and regulators to benefit customers and the industry, along with a willingness to work on some of the fundamental structural and regulatory challenges in the industry for the good of the industry.

---

[7] The definition of the retail channel for this book includes traditional retail branches staffed by loan officers, builder and realtor owned mortgage lenders, joint ventures between a lender and a real estate broker, builder, wealth managers and the use of bank branches for a bank owned lender to make mortgage loans.

During interviews, several CEOs noted that many retail mortgage bankers' processes and workflows are front-end origination-centric. Several hypotheses were put forth. Loan officers who have success, become a branch manager, and then start their own mortgage banking companies tend to be very originator-centric. As a strategy, it's all about getting the deal in the door and then doing whatever it takes to get the deal closed. In conversation, this sounds like an effective customer service strategy. In practice, however, this sometimes leads to process accommodations for 'rush' files, special handling for VIP customers, lots of rework and resubmissions, and much angst at the end of each month's push to get loan closings done.

I had a discussion with a very originator-centric CEO regarding the speed of closing for various loan characteristics. The CEO suggested that high credit metric loans were moving quickly and efficiently through the process. The 'tough' deals were much slower because of extensive underwriter touches, the need for more documentation, more conditions from AUS, etc. On the surface, it sounded like it made sense.

Here are the actual metrics:

CREDIT METRICS	APPLICATION TO LOAN CLOSE DAYS	APPLICATION TO INVESTOR FUNDING DAYS
FICO < 640; LTV> 90%, DTI > 40%	43	61
FICO >740; LTV< 70%, DTI < 31%	42	60
All other loans	43	61
Lender Average	42	61
Standard Deviation	19	20

These statistics made little sense to the CEO. The first explanation offered by the CEO was that purchase transactions take longer to close regardless of credit metrics, so "tough" purchase loans take as long as "slam dunk" purchase loans. Further analysis found that the number of file touches and resubmissions was similar for all three groups of loans, and that the time to the "clear to close" milestone was not changed by credit metrics. At that point, the CEO suggested the data was incorrect. It wasn't; the dataset was extracted from the lender's systems by a profit intelligence tool. The LOS is the "system of record" that held all the dates, data, and characteristics.

Interestingly, these statistics were never presented to the CEO by his staff, though the data was contained within the lender's systems. The operations executives also argued the statistics were incorrect and misleading. In fact, the statistics were not flattering to the CEO's management team and, after a series of discussions, the data was again begrudgingly verified as correct by the operations management. The CEO was angry that these "sins of omission" left him with a distorted view of operational efficiency.

Significantly, the standard deviations were fairly large at 19 and 20 days respectively to consumer close and investor funding. Some loans took over 100 days to fund. This goes back to the Florida versus Death Valley statistical dispersion discussion. 42 days to close is close to peer average, but the standard deviation suggested some loans took much longer, while some were shorter. More like Death Valley temperatures. And when a loan takes longer than promised, the customer becomes very uncomfortable and unhappy, and tells their friends, family, and social media connections.

A deeper dive into the data looked at loan officer/processor/underwriter/closer times to close. The variations were startling to me (and to the CEO). Further review found that the lending process was loosely defined, that branches had their own various methods of originating loans, the quality of application was very varied by loan officer and branch, and the culture was "get it closed". In some cases, the branches were able to work very effectively. In others, the result was operational chaos at the end of the month, especially in the centralized closing function. The variation on application to investor funding was very dependent on the combination of loan officer/processor/underwriter/closer. Some combinations worked very well, some did not. Rather than having a defined company-wide process, each branch and employee found their own method of working with a very loosely defined process. In some cases, this worked well. In other cases, it did not.

In branches where it did not work well, the costs were concessions, cures, and operational labor that consumed about 30-80 basis points more than peer. The overall impact on this lender's profitability was severe. In a good quarter, lender profitability was about 25% of the MBA peer group[8]. That's a high price to pay for a poorly designed lender-wide process and workflow.

There is more empirical evidence of a poorly defined process affecting actual lender viability. A client engaged our company to help with an LOS migration from an in-house system. The lender was moderately sized, with about 60 branches. Two weeks into the deal, after several very intense conversations with the lender's leadership, we decided the business process could not be effectively transformed. It was clear that the vision was "keep

---

[8] The reader will note that this book uses a 'data driven' approach when addressing process, workflow, technology and financial results. In my view, this data driven approach provides objective insights that supplement the subjective discussions herein.

the loan officers happy", the culture was totally branch-centric, and the new LOS would be implemented with a great deal of diversity among branches to the point that there would be little defined process or workflow – in other words, 60 different ways of doing things. The extreme diversity almost guaranteed high levels of variability (high standard deviation) in process, and much time to correct documentation and underwriting defects, as well as an unacceptable number of unsalable loans. It's very hard to tell a client we can't help, and I've only had to do it a few times. Unfortunately for the lender, our assessment proved correct and the lender no longer exists.

In another case, a FinTech lender had a clear vision of their marketing and technology strategy, but no experience closing loans. The FinTech leadership had little understanding of the complex nature of mortgage banking and the systems necessary for compliant and profitable mortgage lending operations. They had great data scientists and a visionary CEO, but few experienced mortgage bankers and little understanding of the customer experience issues that would arise from fundamental weaknesses in basic strategy, process, and workflow. Reputation is everything, and the engagement leader suggested we step away to protect ours, which we did.

These examples are not intended as critique but put forth simply as emblematic of the cause and effect of attempting to implement process, workflow, and technology before first settling on an effective vision, culture, and customer experience. While branch and loan officer centricity are a vision, taken to the extreme it results in chaos. Same for FinTech front ends. The experience can be almost Amazon-like in look and feel, but fulfillment processes and regulatory compliance must be equal partners in that experience to avoid an unprofitable business model.

While a detailed discussion of vision and culture are beyond the scope of this book, virtually all the maverick CEOs interviewed could articulate their vision and culture, customer experience, process, workflow, and technology strategy, and they were clear on one thing—the desired customer experience.

Putting the Customer First

As a starting point, most of these maverick thought leaders began with a customer experience-centered approach. The clear majority of the CEOs I spoke with were extraordinarily involved in customer experience and viewed customer satisfaction as the central motivator behind their companies. These maverick CEOs recognized that the careful end-to-end mortgage banking process and workflow design created superior customer satisfaction. Many maverick CEOs related that their focus on customer service was a never-ending journey and, moreover, that resting on achievement was a sure way to be bypassed. Want proof?

The 2012 J.D. Power Mortgage Origination Customer Satisfaction Survey[9] winner was the only lender to score over 800 customer satisfaction points, with a winning score of 817. No other lender scored over 800 in the 2012 Survey. The winning score in 2016 was 869. Eighteen other lenders scored over 800 in 2016. The

[9] The J.D. Power U.S. Primary Mortgage Origination Satisfaction Study (SM) examines customer satisfaction with the origination experience among the largest mortgage lenders in the United States. The study provides a broad understanding of how firms can improve mortgage customer satisfaction, loyalty, and advocacy across six key factors: Loan Offerings, Application/Approval Process, Interaction, Closing, Onboarding and Problem Resolution. The survey results are reported separately for loan origination activities and loan servicing activities.

number one winning score of 817 from 2012 now scores thirteenth in 2016. Ever-increasing customer expectations by and large leads to an overall strategic plan that is also customer-focused and—perhaps most importantly—is executed by an intentionally created corporate culture backed up by process, workflow, and technology, all with the goal of delivering exceptional service levels and financial results.

The J.D. Power survey is not the decisive metric on customer satisfaction for all lenders, since participants in the survey are limited to national, high-volume lenders. Whether via the J.D. Power survey or other measurement and survey techniques, virtually all maverick CEOs measured customer satisfaction in at least one manner. That measurement could be a formal net promoter score, a third-party provider customer satisfaction measurement services, anonymous scoring of a questionnaire asking, "How did we do?", "Will you recommend us?", etc. The key element was the maverick CEO's desire to obtain feedback from the customer about "how well did we do". The main reason cited by maverick CEOs on formally measuring customer satisfaction: Employees need to know that customer satisfaction is important, that it is measured objectively, and that it is very important to the CEO. As one maverick CEO said, "You get what you measure."

Why measure customer satisfaction formally? According to several CEOs, the main reason was to filter out internal feedback. Ask a loan production management executive, "How are we doing?' and the answer is "Great!" Ask operations, "How are we doing?" ... The answer is "Great! Turnaround time is better than industry average". We've discussed the Death Valley issue of "industry averages" and variation in turnaround time. I'm sure these comments resonate with you, since I heard the same from my team in my twenty-five years of lending at three lenders, the most recent of which was one of the top 50 lenders[10] in the U.S.

At my own companies, we were serious about the vision and culture. Our promise to customers was on all marketing and company materials, including every business card of every employee: "We Help People Buy, Afford and Enjoy the Home of Their Dreams" which we trademarked in 2005[11]. The promise was used often to ensure clarity of purpose with all our team: The question wasn't whether we make the loan or sell the loan to an investor. The key question was whether the borrower could *afford and enjoy the home of their dreams*. It wasn't enough to ensure they could buy the home—our team had to engage collectively with the *"buy, afford, and enjoy"*. We gave up much business (and had loan production branches resign) in 2005-2007 during the subprime boom. We believed subprime loans with negative amortization, 2/28 payment shock risk, no-doc, etc. violated our promise of *"afford and enjoy"*. A borrower doesn't enjoy a home when the borrower is facing payment shock, late payments, and foreclosure.

---

[10] American Home Bank N.A. was chartered as a start-up in 2001; the Bank primarily followed a residential lending strategy as a seller/servicer. The Bank grew to closing about 20,000 mortgage loans per year, as well as lending in the commercial real estate and construction lending space. The Bank had eight joint ventures with builders and realtors. We sold the Bank to a publicly traded bank holding company, and by successor via merger, BB&T now owns resulting merged entity. According to S&P Market Intelligence Service, "American Home Bank, National Association provides residential financial services in the new construction market in the United States. The company operates in the retail, wholesale, and correspondent mortgage businesses, as well as joint venture mortgage partnerships with builders and manufacturers. Its services include consumer/commercial banking, online banking, mortgage lending, and construction lending and building services."

[11] US Patent and Trademark Office Registration Number 31711915, "We Help People Buy, Afford and Enjoy the Home of Their Dreams".

To measure how well the process delivered our promise, we used a customer survey questionnaire post-settlement. The last question was: "Would you recommend us to a family member or friend?" If the answer was "no", we asked for more details. We called every customer with a "no" to find out how we could make it right. We celebrated the originators with the highest customer recommendation rates. The competitive nature of many in the business resulted in many originators achieving 98, 99% or in some cases 100% satisfaction rates, with recognition and rewards attached to high "will recommend" rates.

This survey was put in place *well* before Dodd-Frank. Like many service level standards, there needs to be rewards for superior results, and discipline for failure. To put teeth in our customer service metrics, every "will not recommend" meant the loan officer, processor, closer, and anyone on commission or bonus was not paid on a "will not recommend" response. This approach pushed "will recommend" rates to 98% company-wide. While Dodd-Frank made directly linking loan level performance to loan level incentive a casualty of federal regulation, one can still vary compensation on quality and satisfaction basis on a broader level, not linked to a specific transaction.

One of the most insightful conversations I had around this issue was with Bill Emerson at Quicken Loans, a company that is now famous for its culture in the industry. Their popular "Quicken-ISMs"—sayings that the company lives by and encourages the team to live by—have become, to many, emblematic of what it means to focus on and foment culture with an eye on customer experience.

When asked about why Quicken came out at the top again and again when it comes to customer satisfaction, Bill responded point blank, "It's just the culture of the organization." Culture at Quicken is a work in progress and characterized by their now world-famous ISMs. Naturally, Bill cited one of these famed ISMs in our discussion on customer satisfaction and culture:

> *"Every client. Every time. No exceptions. No excuses."* He elaborated with, *"You really can't live any other way if you're going to be in a retail lending environment ... I think that the [industry] belief was that you really can't give high touch service in a centralized model. Frankly nothing can be further from the truth because, at the end of the day, it's really about how you treat a client, how responsive you are to that client."*

Quicken's record has shown that this isn't just talk. High touch service is possible by leveraging technology, and it can garner outstanding results in the retail lending environment.

Susan Stewart of SWBC echoed much of this sentiment, stressing the importance of tuning into the customer. "The feedback is coming in all the time... are you listening?" This human element works on two levels when it comes to culture, according to Susan. The human touch, for one, allows for self-learning and improvement— "Are you willing to look at what you're doing perpetually and change it?" On another level, the human element keeps the right ethos at a company and the right people on a team. Susan's ethos includes "Be nice to be nice. Or be nice because it's good business." Said another way, abusive individuals were not to be tolerated. "You can mess up and keep your job, but be a jerk and you're fired."

How can other companies achieve this? Two common themes came out of the discussions I had with maverick CEOs regarding culture and technology. First, technology doesn't come first—the culture does. (As does the definition of customer experience, process and workflow.) Second, one needs to start at the back end of the loan manufacturing process when deploying technology, not at the front end. Let's explore each theme.

Understanding Technology's Place

From my perspective on the industry, culture is a combination of overall vision *coupled with* the customer experience that a company wants to deliver to its customers (and with the resulting parameters of high profitability, low cost, employee retention and defect free loan files). Deb Still of Pulte described it as having to develop a borrower relationship with emotional attachment while using technology to make the process more efficient. This efficiency lets Pulte employees have the time to connect with borrowers and build professional relationships that are also stitched together with the emotional attachment of Pulte employees helping the customer achieve their homeownership dream. In Deb's words, "it's all about connecting vision and purpose—after all, the joy of home ownership should get you out of bed in the morning." Technology serves the customer experience and helps fulfill Pulte's strategy.

Deb Still is not alone. Virtually all the CEOs felt that technology was an adjunct tool to the process of building a relationship with the customer. Not one felt that the entire mortgage lending process should or could be automated.

It goes without saying—the mortgage process is very complex. Over fifty pages of disclosures are provided to the customer, and the average loan file has grown to hundreds of pages. The qualification process, documentation process, terms, and conditions are just too complex for a completely automated solution. At some point in the process (and usually at more than one point), a borrower wants trusted advice, whether face to face or via electronic interaction. Indeed, both Quicken and Pulte use a direct to consumer strategy in which it is rare for the borrower actually to meet an employee of the lender face to face. Trusted relationships *can* be effectively formed at a distance.

Larry Flowers, CEO of Northside Bank in Georgia, suggested a chart[12] that illustrates the increase in the complexity of loan file documentation. "The visual impact is powerful." Larry added, "Does anyone actually think more paper improves the file quality or borrower understanding of their transaction?" More paper makes the need for trusted relationships even more important.

LOAN FILE PAGE COUNT

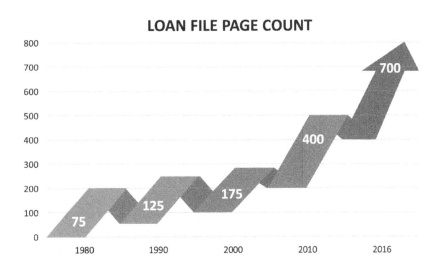

<hr />

[12] The chart is illustrative and was Larry Flowers' interpretation of loan file size. It appears directionally correct to me.

Complexity and excess paperwork are also why many CEOs suggest that a lender begin fulfilling its strategy and the customer experience by starting at the end of the process. As Steven Covey said in "7 Habits", begin with the end in mind. My interpretation of Covey's work as it related to the lending process is to begin at the end, with the customer experience in mind.

Beginning at the end of the process also exposes the fallacy of speaking about the loan "manufacturing process". It's rarely a manufacturing process in the truest sense. And that's why it costs so much to originate a loan.

Jerry Schiano of New Penn Financial said,

> *If you look at an underwriter in a conventional first mortgage business, they do two loans a day. In managing that business, I don't understand that. Is it the legacy requirements of the secondary market? And the agency investors? Is the industry just unwilling to change?*
>
> *The second issue is there's too much complexity. The products are different, and guidelines constantly change. You have to do something differently than a year ago. You have to do something different for jumbo investors.*
>
> *The third problem is the mortgage business process. And I think this is where people like Blend will make a difference. Mortgages start out with the sales people. And the sales people don't start the process well enough. Whether that be because they haven't been trained properly or their systems are problematic, there's never been anyone who says, 'I love my origination system'.*

Many of the CEOs I've spoken with stress the need to envision strategy and customer experience as "what it is" and "what it is not". What it should be is easy, seamless, fast, intuitive and self-correcting.

What it should *not be* has been well documented by J.D. Power. "Overall satisfaction scores have increased year over year, but a high percentage of home buyers are remorseful about their mortgage lender selection, according to the J.D. Power 2016 U.S. Primary Mortgage Origination Satisfaction[13] Study. (SM) The study shows that 21% of customers purchasing a home express regret over their choice of lender, and 27% of first-time home buyers regret their choice. The reasons for low satisfaction include:

- Higher incidence of problems during the loan process;

- Lack of communication;

- Unmet promises;

- Having to "jump through hoops" to get the loan closed.

The survey also highlighted growing acceptance of customer embracing technology: over 40% of customers indicating they completed some or all of their detailed loan application online in 2017, up from 22% in 2015 and 18% in 2014. This is not necessarily the effect of consumer direct lending. Many borrowers elect to provide information to a retail lender by providing information online, while still having a relationship face to face or telephonically with a loan officer.

---

[13] http://www.jdpower.com/press-releases/jd-power-2016-us-primary-mortgage-origination-satisfaction-study

Importantly, customer satisfaction measurement isn't concluded when the loan closes. The servicing transfer and loan onboarding to a servicer can impact customer satisfaction. The following items detract from customer satisfaction and a seamless process, as highlighted by J.D. Power's 2017 Loan Servicing survey[14]:

- **Long Waits** – 1 in 10 consumers feels their time is wasted when they engage with their mortgage servicer, and satisfaction drops by a huge margin when consumers feel their time is being wasted.

- **Inefficient Onboarding** - Consumer satisfaction declines when the onboarding process is not fast, efficient, and seamless.

- **No Digital Access** - Consumer satisfaction is 40+ points lower when the borrower does not have access to a website during the servicing process.

Lenders who release servicing may put the overall satisfaction on the loan transaction at risk (and out of their control) when a loan servicer does not set up the loan flawlessly or is hard to communicate with.

The Crucial Metric - Customer Satisfaction

Quicken, SWBC, and some others achieve high customer satisfaction. Yet among the 10,000 banks, credit unions, thrifts and independent mortgage bankers in the United States, few companies in the mortgage industry plan and create the value chain to deliver consistent satisfaction and repeat business.

[14] http://www.jdpower.com/press-releases/jd-power-2017-us-primary-mortgage-servicer-satisfaction-study

In some ways, it may be a result of the cultural resistance in the industry I've already mentioned, including the idea that "if we build it, they will come." When I spoke with Jamie Korus-Pearce, President of Alliance Home Loans, she stressed the importance of moving away from a self-serving vision for a company. "We're not here just to generate profit." She stressed that she envisions success at a company as stemming from an understanding that the team is helping customers to build a future and build safer, better lives for their families—the ultimate vision of her Company is to serve as a tool that helps impact customers in a very positive way.

At this point, it is important to point out that my research for this book was not limited to the 25 maverick CEOs identified by name. I also spoke to more than fifty "C" level executives at a variety of lenders[15]. Some of these lenders were high-performing, some were struggling with profitability and/or customer satisfaction. In some of my conversations during the development of this book, I also saw some resistance to the technological innovation in demand by the modern consumer, though I heard far more enthusiasm overall. This

---

[15] My discussions with thought leading maverick CEOs needed to be balanced by discussions with CEOs that I felt may not be 'thought leaders'. While this was a subjective classification, 'thought leading' CEOs seemed to have higher customer satisfaction, higher satisfaction among employees and higher profitability. It should be highlighted that most 'non-thought' leading CEOs ran solid organizations that most observers would consider successful, though not able to scale. A third group of CEOs in my research group had either literally run a company into failure, conservatorship, or significant regulatory or financial difficulties. This third group was an effective contrast to the thought leader group. Finally, I spoke with about 25 non-financial services executives for their perspectives, including Gary Kelly, CEO of Southwest Airlines; Andrew Liveris, CEO of Dow Chemical; Steve Shank of Flinchbaugh Engineering, Inc.; Jeffrey Immelt, now former CEO of General Electric; Duncan L. Niederauer, now former CEO of the New York Stock Exchange; James Lockhart III of W.L. Ross & Co.; and Governor Rick Scott (Florida) as example executives comprising this group. Some conversation with this final group were compact, some were extensive, and all were impactful.

may be a "front of the house" versus "back of the house" culture war and could also be old guard versus new. Whatever is driving it, it is clear most that voices are calling for technological innovation and that this goes hand in hand with increasing customer satisfaction.

Let's dive into this in detail. When it comes to customer satisfaction in mortgage banking, what are our gauges? What should we measure, and when and how should we do it? Furthermore, what are the technological innovations that will keep new customers engaged?

Technology and the Consumer

What surveys have shown again and again in recent years is that more and more borrowers are turning to online applications. Some in the industry call it the "Digital Mortgage", though so far that is a loosely defined term.

In 2014, according to J.D. Power, just 14% of borrowers filled out some or all of their application online. As of 2017, that number was up to 44% - a more than significant uptick. The mortgage banking industry should expect this number to continue to increase significantly and plan accordingly.

Working hand in hand with consumer demand for online access is that the new generation of borrowers—the Millennials—are extremely tech-savvy. Plus, they have high expectations. These expectations are not just about being able to fill out an application online but involve something that doesn't necessarily come naturally to mortgage banking—**the instant answer.** A recent survey by Forrester indicated that a whopping 57% of consumers were likely to abandon a purchase entirely if an answer to a question was not immediately forthcoming. And this instant answer standard is not just applicable to online experience. It's also expected in face-to-face or phone conversations.

So, what to do? For one, mortgage banking needs to focus on streamlined, fast, user-friendly online experiences. Creating an ideal digital mortgage experience[16] is, of course, no easy task. That's where BeSmartee, Blend, Roostify, SimpleNexus and others provide value. Today's consumers demand very specific things from a business's digital presence:

- Quick answers to questions

- Quick access to information

- Self-service

- Engagement

The first two are perhaps the easiest to address. A comprehensive source of answers to common questions, for one, is the most basic (and essential) starting point to giving the modern consumer incentive to proceed with the lender. Many lenders miss many of the basic questions: What is the process? What happens next after I fill out these forms? How do I contact you? How do I want you to contact me? Some thought leaders use short videos for putting a human face on the lender to begin building the relationship. Some use a web-based process walk-through. Some use traditional, written FAQs.

---

[16] "Digital Mortgage Experience" is still an evolving term and means different things to different parties. My use here is to loosely describe the self-service, online process from Initial Consumer Interest to Application.

But are questions that easy to answer when it comes to mortgages? As my daughter's experience testified to, even knowing *where in the process one is* sometimes seems impossible. It seems clear that effective customer service in mortgage banking cannot only involve FinTech, but needs to bring together new technologies with a new, digitally transformed mortgage process. Is this achievable? In later chapters, we will discuss each in detail.

Beyond that, an effective digital mortgage experience for customer service is not the only way to go. If a question comes up that a borrower cannot answer readily online[17], mortgage bankers may need to provide effective online customer service via live employees or Virtual Agent/Intelligent Agent technology.

Navigating Social

We will discuss self-service in a moment, which is a multi-layered issue. Engagement, however, is straightforward and perhaps not the most intuitive process for mortgage bankers. Today's consumers, especially Millennials, are virtually guaranteed to share what they think about their mortgage banking experience on social media.

Lenders may be vocal about the Consumer Financial Protection Bureau (CFPB)'s "complaint database" but may not be as sensitive to negative information posted on social media. Quicken is the undisputed leader in customer satisfaction. But a Google search of "Quicken Loans Sucks" returns 210,000 results, some of which are not very flattering. Consider searching [your company's name] "sucks", or a similar unflattering adjective. See a

[17] Throughout this book, "web" and "online" mean collectively web and mobile access.

little further in this chapter if your search yields more than a few unflattering results.

Some think of loan manufacturing technology and social media as separate platforms. Amazon has melded their sales and operational platform with their social media platform and formed a community within their single application. The typical process for mortgage lending is set out below from Initial Consumer Interest in a loan through Funding by the end investor purchasing the loan. The process often transcends several platforms: A Customer Relationship Management system, Loan Origination System, a Quality Assurance system. Where does social media fit in? Is it confined to the "shop" and "compare" functions? Does social media span the whole process? What about servicing and retention?

CUSTOMER INITIAL INTEREST TO APPLICATION				APPLICATION TO CLOSING						
Shop	Compare	Pricing & Loan Types	Application & Disclosures	Processing	Underwriting	Prefunding QC	Closing	Post-Closing	Shipping & Condition Clearance	Funding

What does this mean for the highly regulated and serious mortgage banking industry? It means acknowledging and accepting that social is king for a growing percentage of mortgage customers. The industry needs to prioritize this conversation, and individual companies need to take part in the conversation for the sake of customer satisfaction and *to learn* from this conversation for the sake of customer service. An ever-increasing group of customers share their experiences on social media, and a variety of customer research firms note that an unhappy customer will share their frustration with customer service nine times more often than will a satisfied customer share a positive experience. It is very important to identify and engage with dissatisfied customers *on a systemic basis*. A lender needs to prevent a dissatisfied customer from remaining dissatisfied as quickly as possible. If left uncorrected, these negative comments are shared not only with the customer's associates, but also end up on social media, and can then be transported to a very wide audience through search engines and social sites.

Look up your company by name on Yelp, Zillow, Glass Door, Indeed, as well as Facebook, Twitter, and other social media. A *systemic response process* needs to be part of your business process and workflow. An unsatisfied customer? Get out in front and engage quickly, before the dissatisfaction spreads to various social media and is cataloged on search engines. Consider a process that permits employees to elevate a customer who appears to be becoming very dissatisfied for remedial executive communication. It could be something as simple as a supervisor or manager calling the customer and asking how the loan process is working for them. But it must *be systemic*. Similarly, if your process and workflow does not have *a systemic* dissatisfied customer remediation element, you risk having very poor reviews on social media that are not challenged.

I often use Yelp or OpenTable to find a restaurant when I'm traveling. The overall rating is important, but I read the individual reviews and search for zero or one-star ratings. (I'm always looking for the Death Valley variance effect.) I read these comments and note whether the restaurant has responded to the negative review. If the restaurant has responded, many times the customer is appreciative and will give the restaurant another try (and often upgrades the review). If there is no response, it suggests to me that these reviews should be given credence.

I generally only post social media comments for particularly excellent or poor experiences. My wife and I recently had dinner with friends in Boston. I picked the place. The dinner was unimpressive, and my usually very tolerant wife suggested I post a review, which follows:

> *Our evening started with a grumpy hostess that told us to stand in the entranceway until a table was ready, despite having a reservation. Appetizers were unimpressive, (Pasta Faggioli that was not notable and iceberg lettuce with a brown covering advertised as a Caesar Salad). Entrees were average at best, though the veal special with fresh mozzarella was the highpoint of the evening. Wine was expensive and served warm in nice Walmart style wine glasses, which added a touch of ambiance. Bill including tip was $200 for 4 people without dessert. Look elsewhere.*

The restaurant never responded or reached out to me. I'll never go back, even though business brings me to the Boston area frequently.

A key takeaway for CEOs—if you don't have a systemic process to identify dissatisfied customers and remediate their source of dissatisfaction, you are missing a key element in the lending process. From experience, when I reached out to my company's borrowers who completed our survey with "will not recommend to family member or friend", the phone call usually started with the customer's surprise that an executive called based on the survey, and that the executive would ask, "How can we make this right?" At the end of the call, the remediation promised was set in motion. But more often than not, the customer said the outreach changed their view of the company. In a few instances, the customers became some of our best promoters when they tell the story of "I complained, and the CEO called and made it right".

And when making calls to dissatisfied customers, make sure you require that an executive with authority to resolve the issue actually makes the call. Handling very dissatisfied customers is not the work of front line staff without authority. A side benefit is that executives hear exactly what the customer thinks, and why they think it. It's humbling to hear how we failed to deliver, but offering to fix a customer's complaint, as well as acting to address the root cause of the issue, can be the best use of an executive's time.

Getting back to social media and customer experience in a mortgage banking world, as with everything in mortgage banking, federal guidelines inform the experience, so to speak. For the intrepid loan officer or company looking to build relationships on social media, guidance provided by the Federal Financial Institutions Examination Council in 2013 may make things more complicated.[18] It seems even social media becomes a discussion of "risk assessment" and requires a "risk management program" when it comes to mortgage banking. As well as executive vigilance.

I often Google a sample of loan officers when we consider taking on a new client. It's interesting to see how the loan officer uses the official company online presence, as well as how they leverage other social media content. One of the more unusual post that came up at one point was a loan officer of a potential client in a strip club, with a group of his purported referral sources toasting to a good time with loosely clad strip club hostesses. For a variety of reasons, we did not work with this client. While the strip club picture was not a good omen, regulatory cease and desist orders for loan officers and loan officer state debarments found with a Google search of other company loan officers suggested that this potential client

---

[18] https://www.fdic.gov/news/news/financial/2013/fil13056.html

had very loose recruiting due diligence. Not a good reputational fit for our company.

As everyone across the mortgage banking space looks more and more into enhancing the customer experience, we may find again and again that governmental guidelines and regulations complicate the works.

Freeing the Consumer

With regards to self-service, one interesting metric to parse is the fact that borrowers are feeling *forced* into choices. Being forced into a choice is anathema for Millennials, at least, who want to be able to initiate and execute purchases autonomously and in an instant via mobile. Beyond the tech savvy, however, many mortgage consumers have expressed frustration with the lack of freedom they experience during the loan process.

The 2016 J.D. Power Mortgage Origination Survey[SM] showed that nearly three-quarters of borrowers who reported high customer satisfaction still felt that they had been pressured by lenders into choosing a particular loan product. While these pressures may be informed by necessity, "mortgage banker knows best" doesn't have quite the ring that "doctor knows best" does. This finding sets off alarm bells in my head, as "feeling pressure to use a particular loan product" is high on the list of federal regulators as an undesirable attribute at best, and "steering" at its worst.

What can the industry do to make this particular pain point easier for the consumer?

From J.D. Power: "This 'happy buyer's remorse is in part due to customers feeling that circumstances out of their control drove them to a particular choice and that options weren't totally clear," said Craig Martin, director of the mortgage practice at J.D. Power. "Like a lot of consumers, they are happy with a good deal, but they can feel that they have to jump through hoops to get the deal. In the end, they may not fully understand exactly what they got, and the longer-term risk for lenders is that customers' perceptions of the deal may change in the future."

Being aware of unintended experiences of customers informs a lender of how to script 'reducing pressure' into the process, workflow and tasks within the lender's overall customer experience design. Consider this as part of a company's overall risk management process.

'Jumping through hoops' is exactly the type of pain point FinTech on the consumer end can ameliorate. We will look at FinTech in greater detail further on in the book, but for now, it bears mentioning within the conversation on customer service and satisfaction. And remember when considering the mortgage banking customer experience, *begin with the end in mind.* Start at the end of the mortgage banking process (servicing/securitization) and work forward to the beginning point—Initial customer interest in a mortgage—as a method for digitally transforming your mortgage lending process.

CHAPTER TWO

Expanding the
Access to Credit

A s I rode in an Uber with Samir in New York City, we struck up a conversation. Samir was married and appeared to be in his late twenties or early thirties. Samir related that he drove for a Yellow Cab operator, Uber, Lyft, delivered food for Seamless (a multi-restaurant food delivery service), helped a friend from time to time as an apartment doorman, and did some handy man work. "I have to work hard," he said.

Samir was a first-generation immigrant working hard to build his dream in the U.S. He was saving money. His dream included buying a home of his own for his family. He said, however, he wasn't sure he could get a loan for a home. I wondered how I would qualify him for a mortgage, if I were a loan officer.

A similar experience occurred in Toronto. I rode with cab driver Ibrahim, a Pakistani with a computer science degree from Florida State University. He attended college on a student visa. He worked for a year in Florida as a programmer for a technology company.

The subprime crisis hit, he was laid off, and then had to leave the United States as his work visa expired.

Ibrahim came to Canada under a Temporary Foreign Worker Program to drive a cab. He was saving money, working hard, hoping to become a Canadian citizen in about three years. He then planned to get a U.S. visa as a Canadian citizen. "It is much easier to get a visa to the U.S. as a Canadian citizen." He planned to work at a technology company in the U.S. "Why the U.S.?" I asked. I'll never forget his answer. He turned to me, smiled, and said, "The U.S. is the only country in the world that will give me a chance to own my home. I want to own a piece of America. In Florida."

Samir and Ibrahim likely represent one of many large cohorts of potential first-time homebuyers that aren't like the first-time homebuyers from the Baby Boomer wave of late 1960s and 1970s.

Family formation is perhaps the strongest driver of the economy, as it generates the need for shelter, transportation, and furnishings, among other things. Family formation is largely driven by demographics, which are propelled by births and immigration, as well as the time dimension.

The following chart shows family formation over a fifty year period.

AVERAGE ANNUAL HOUSEHOLD FORMATION
(in Thousands)

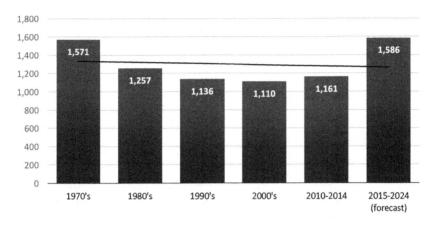

The takeaway is that average annual household formation will approach the level of the 1970s (when baby boomers hit their demographically-driven family formation period). The estimate of 2015-2024 family formation levels hitting about 1.6 million units per year contrasts with the relatively low rate of new housing construction of 500-600,000 units over the previous ten years. This shortfall in new housing stock is being felt today. Inventories of homes for sale are low, particularly at the entry level.

High cost areas such as the California Bay Area, New York City, Los Angeles, and other areas have regulatory limits on new construction. Regulatory limitations hit builders particularly hard in the form of impact fees, land density requirements, zoning requirements, and land costs. Add the time required to transform raw land to "approved, improved" land ready to build, and one can see the squeeze on homebuilding, particularly at the entry level. As a result, many families (whether a family unit of one or many) currently rent a home.

Kevin Pearson, President of CalAtlantic Mortgage, subsidiary of CalAtlantic Builders, stated, "The price of housing has made it difficult on new construction for our products. It's hard to increase first time homebuyer product going forward. Regulatory requirements add $50 to 80 thousand to just getting each building lot ready to build a house on." Thus, it's hard to build entry-level housing in many locations, since the cost of land drives the total home price above "entry level".

According to Mike Fratantoni, Chief Economist of the Mortgage Bankers Association of America, net immigration currently accounts for almost half of U.S. population growth. Census projects the U.S. population will grow at the fastest rate of the G10 countries. Finally, immigration has recently accounted for most of the growth in the working-age population.[19] This translates into needing to meet the credit characteristics as well as the cultural norms of those immigrant families seeking shelter.

Patty Arvielo noted that Hispanic borrowers "are very family oriented and culturally the family unit is supreme." It is not unusual to have three or more generations in one household[20]. This cultural trend does not fit neatly into easy access for credit on several dimensions. First, not all potential homebuyers fit neatly into a credit score-driven credit model. Patty noted that family ties will often result in intergenerational and familial financial assistance needed by one family member.

This cultural benefit doesn't translate into a dimension of Dodd-Frank Ability to Qualify regulations. Nor does it serve immigrants

---

[19] Mike Fratantoni, at MBA Midwinter Conference Presentation, March 2017.

[20] http://www.jdpower.com/press-releases/jd-power-2017-us-primary-mortgage-servicer-satisfaction-study

who may not have established a scorable credit history but are industrious and are connected to a family network of support.

This cultural phenomenon is not just notable in Hispanic family units. I have personal experience assisting a lender with an overzealous federal banking regulator who insisted loans made in Brooklyn to primarily Chinese-Americans were unsafe and unsound because the income in pre-2010 loans was stated, and that multiple generations of family members were used for qualification. The regulator ignored the 25-40% cash down payment. I pointed out that the OCC's quarterly mortgage statistics indicated that "prime" loans at the time had a 3% serious delinquency rate, and the client's portfolio delinquency was under 2%. A reference to the OCC's Uniform Retail Credit Classification policy stated that "the best evidence of a loan's quality is its payment record." Finally, a "friendly" call to the Assistant Deputy Controller at the OCC duty station eventually solved the issue, but much time and energy was wasted by inappropriate application of a regulatory mindset. This regulatory mindset, however, is one of the reasons that little Non-Qualified Mortgage ("non-QM") lending takes place. And this regulatory mindset reduces credit formation, particularly in first generation immigrants and other groups.

The chart below shows the large increase in rental households:

CHANGE IN OWNER AND RENTER OCCUPIED HOUSEHOLDS & HOMEOWNERSHIP RATE
(Years 1990-2013, In Thousands)

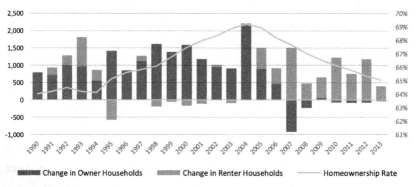

Source: Mortgage Bankers Association and U.S. Census Bureau

The decrease in owner households in 2007 and subsequent years may be tied to the loss of homes to foreclosure resulting from the sub-prime crisis. The large net increase in renters may be tied to tighter mortgage credit, some resistance to homeownership because of the fallout from the subprime crisis, scarcity of single-family housing stock in certain metro areas, and other reasons.

As Julie Piepho of Cornerstone noted, not all family formations and Millennials aspire to homeownership. The needs of renters are equally important in considering shelter needs. Some of the needs are driven by economics of geography. For instance, my son and his wife live in the San Francisco Bay area, where renting is the most logical option, given the cost of shelter for a young family with one child and one on the way. Mobility also plays into the decision to rent. A home in the Palo Alto area that seems large enough for two children is $1.6 to $2.5 million. The transaction costs[21] into and out of a home approach 10%, or about $160,000-$250,000. The likelihood of employment mobility and the high entry cost in many locales drives many Millennials into renting for a period of time—perhaps for a long time.

Cody Pearce of Cascade notes that many families seeking affordable shelter may rent or purchase non-traditional home units such as manufactured housing. In many high cost and remote locations, manufactured housing may represent the best option for shelter for a family unit. Cascade has undertaken a business model to serve these clients with affordable and fast financing for non-real estate loans (i.e. chattel loans, meaning the loan is not real property but rather is titled by the state motor vehicle department). Mr. Pearce shared aggregated, anonymized credit data characteristics of targeted market customers with me; the borrower profile with respect to credit score and DTI would fit into the GSE credit box, but the collateral does not easily fit. Nonetheless, Cascade provides a manufactured housing homeowner the ability to own his or her home—just not the land underneath the home.

Several lenders are specializing in finance for small investment properties. For example, Angel Oak Companies offer innovative investor rehab and permanent financing options to increase the stock of quality rental units. As Steven Schwalb, CEO and Managing Partner of Angel Oak Home Loans said, "We're constantly finding innovative ways to develop outside the box products that are valuable to our clients." In a discussion with Mr. Schwalb, this innovative spirit emerges with loan products aimed at the non-QM space. "Done properly, these loans perform well and are in the consumer's

---

[21] Realtor commissions, lender costs and fees, taxes and governmental fees, etc.

interest." Small investment property rehab and acquisition financing, as well as multi-unit financing, help address the needs of customers seeking rental shelter, as opposed to home ownership.

Student debt is a significant factor for Millennials that can also delay or impede the purchase of a home. The Ability to Repay ("ATR") requirements of Dodd-Frank factor student debt into the total debt ratio for mortgage qualification purposes. With almost $1 trillion of student debt outstanding, the burden on Millennial income to pay student debt is considerable. The GSEs have provided some flexibility on student debt within their AUS engines; however, non-GSE lenders are stuck with Ability to Repay regulations when considering the level of student debt in affordability ratios, but without flexibility to evaluate the longer term, higher income that results from a college, trade school or professional (i.e., CPA, Attorney, Physician) education. ATR fixes us in the "here and now", future earnings prospects be damned.

Expanding access to credit is not a conversation anyone in or out of the mortgage industry wants to approach lightly after the crisis of 2008. The mortgage industry in particular, having borne much of the "blame" for the crisis, has been hesitant to even consider the discussion in the intervening years. What the industry does have to consider, however, is that the evolving marketplace includes potential homebuyers working in the so-called new "gig" economy for one. As technology transforms the workplace, more and more viable homebuyers are being left out in the cold because their income does not fit the industry's definition of "stable" or "monthly" to a tee. What the industry does need to consider is that these types of homebuyers are going to comprise a larger and larger piece of the marketplace and that, furthermore, ignoring them only limits profitability and growth.

Regulatory Burden

David Motley, 2017 Chairman of the Mortgage Bankers Association and President of Colonial Savings, noted that he was "struck by how the government plays such a huge role in our mortgage finance process. The expansive regulatory structure put in place after the financial crisis in 2008 has really impacted consumers' ability to achieve home ownership. I see regulations and I want to do something about it."

The impact of regulation can be seen in the increasing cost of originating a mortgage:

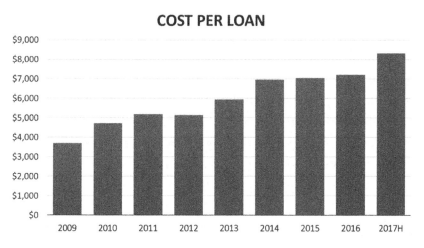

COST PER LOAN

Source: MBA Mortgage Bankers Performance Report

The cost increases include a roughly 50% increase in the number of non-sales personnel at a typical mortgage banker. In 2010, the personnel cost component was approximately 60% in origination personnel and 40% in operations personnel. That mix has reversed. There are now 60% in operations, and 40% in origination.

Said another way, in 2010, a company of 400 employees would have about 240 origination personnel and about 160 operations personnel. In 2017, that same company would have 240 in operations and 160 in origination. Many of the additional operations personnel are compliance focused or are involved in "checking the checkers".

Lenders have had regulators chasing at their heels over the past eight years, and out of necessity have simply added layers to accommodate the added compliance burden. As Jonathan Corr of Ellie Mae has frequently said, applying "human spackle" to cover holes in process doesn't work long term without significant cost impact.

I've seen various estimates of the cost of regulations imposed since 2009—regulations that stem from Dodd-Frank, the Consumer Financial Protection Bureau, and various state regulatory requirements. The estimate of $2,000 per file of increased regulatory burden cost seems about right. For a first-time homebuyer seeking a $160,000 loan, the cost is about 1.3 discount points, which equates to roughly 1/4 to 3/8% in higher interest rate. Would a first-time borrower happily agree to this higher interest rate for "regulatory benefit"? That's $400-$600 per year in increased interest expense, supposedly for "consumer protection".

The $2,000 is before the cost of punitive regulation by enforcement, before the punitive cost of repurchases due to so-called technical defects that were not causal to loan performance, or the costs that the duopoly of Freddie Mac and Fannie Mae imposed via guarantee fee and loan level price adjusters and fees set by regulators, not competition.

Another way to think about this cost is to frame it in terms of a 5% down payment loan typically sought by a first-time buyer. The

$160,000 hypothetical loan down payment is $8,000. Hypothetically, how about a line item on the Loan Estimate that shows additional cash to close of $2,000 for "consumer protection expense"? I favor regulation that is flexible enough to respond to technological and demographic changes; regulation should be subject to cost/benefit analysis and transparency regarding the *cost of the regulation* being borne by consumers. I am not in favor of "hard-coding" elements like debt to income ratio maximums that discourage innovation and assume a legislator can dictate the ratio that "protects" consumers.

This additional cost is borne by the customer in the form of higher interest rates, which increase debt to income and impair the consumer's "ability to repay". I asked consumers anecdotally how much mortgage regulations actually cost them per year; their estimates were way low.

There is also an indirect cost of regulatory uncertainty. David Motley stated, "We need clarity on rules and appropriate penalties for failing to follow them. When we have that, [lenders] will be more willing to lend outside of the four corners of the credit box."

Parsing Ability to Pay

About half of the effort in a mortgage loan file is devoted to verifying and calculating 'stable monthly income'. Stable monthly income has an elevated level of impact because Dodd-Frank regulation after the financial crisis requires lenders to document the "ability to repay" based largely upon documented stable monthly income. Calculation of income for a W-2 employee with the same job for ten years is relatively straight-forward. Computation of self-employed income, particularly contract-employee income with multiple sources of income within a two-year period, is much more difficult. Imagine the look on a processor's face if a loan application from Samir (the Uber drive mentioned above) landed on his or her desk.

Miscalculation of stable monthly income represented about half the defects noted in 2016 by LoanLogics, a provider of quality assurance technology and outsourcing. Fannie, Freddie, and FHA don't make qualifying Samir a particularly easy task.

Like most laws, Dodd-Frank's intentions were good; however, in reality, unanticipated and adverse impact has arisen from these best of intentions. I know of many individuals who have faithfully made mortgage payments on pre- "Ability to Repay" regulation mortgages, who could not qualify today due to documentation requirements.

As I mentioned at the top of this chapter, one of the largest issues now impacting the topic of access to credit is the emergence of two trends: Millennials appear to have a much higher instance of job change and individuals from many generations are engaging in the new gig economy for either full-time or supplemental employment. Using Uber, I've met a dental student, a merchant card services salesperson, a Marriott group sales leader, yellow cab drivers, teachers, and a variety of other interesting individuals.

Many potential borrowers now have non-traditional income sources. Many of the CEOs discussed the difficulty of qualifying potential borrowers with non-traditional employment and income sources. Many first-generation immigrants have multiple jobs, gig economy jobs, multiple part-time jobs, and frequent job changes. These characteristics just don't neatly fit into the "Ability to Repay" requirements. And no consideration is given for a family support network, income mobility, and borrower character.

Think about all the gig economy workers out there now: independent contractors, rideshare drivers, eBayers, handymen, and so on. Most of these workers have no way to document their income as stable monthly income. While the intent of Dodd-Frank was to prevent subprime "liar loans", what it has done in the new gig economy is hold many borrowers to an unfair metric.

This issue has not gone unobserved by thought leaders in the space, either. Dave Stevens, CEO of Mortgage Bankers Association of America, has definitive views on potential borrowers who cannot get credit due to the restrictive documentation standards of Dodd-Frank and the tight credit boxes of the GSEs.

GSE Reform

In my conversation with Dave for this book, he spoke out quite clearly on GSE reform. For Dave, the need for reform is clear, but he also asserts that GSE's need to reframe their ambitions in the marketplace, so to speak. "My view on GSE reform is there needs to be more competition. Because their duopolies don't have an obligation to be transparent with what they do, I think they manage their market share... they are both fairly adverse to credit risk because it's not in their best interests in terms of driving ultimate profits... [T]hey still behave very much like shareholder owned companies even though they're in conservatorship under the umbrella of the US Treasury and FHFA."

In my opinion, the GSE aversion to credit risk weighs on the backs of borrowers. The GSEs use "loan level price adjusters" to increase the price of credit for adverse credit characteristics in borrowers. But the base level of guarantee fees remains in the 35-45 basis point level, despite very low credit losses of just a few basis points in recent years. Said another way, every borrower pays a base guarantee fee that may not be related to actual credit losses of the current period of business. Without being stuck in conservatorship, competitive GSEs would have had to raise equity to replace the losses they incurred from the financial crisis, and then had to price credit risk based on expected performance of the credit book being originated in a competitive marketplace.

The lack of competition, plus the perverse structure of the GSE conservatorship, means normal competitive signals are drowned out by regulatory diktat. The conservatorship reduces competition *and* innovation in the marketplace, since virtually every decision at the GSEs is subject to a lengthy review and approval process. Innovation is stymied as well by the tendency of GSE employees to regard any possible innovation through the lens of "will this be viewed negatively by the conservator's watchdog tasked employees". Not innovation on par with Kelly Johnson's Skunk Works, in the author's opinion. (Johnson worked for Lockheed Aircraft, and with his team of engineers designed over 40 innovative aircraft at a facility he called the "Skunk Works". More on Skunk Works in a later chapter.)

Again, in a lateral way, Dave Stevens touched on transforming culture and taking a more consumer-oriented approach. "They [GSEs] ought to have a more explicit and meaningful duty to serve, [with] access to affordable housing on a broader spectrum." Stevens cites the marked shift in demographics that is set to happen in the next 20 years as a driving force in his thinking. While 70 percent of pre-recession housing stock in the U.S. was owned and occupied by white non-Hispanics, in the next 20 years that will shift dramatically to 70 percent owned and occupied by non-whites, according to MBA's White Paper, "GSE Reform: *Creating a Sustainable, More Vibrant, Secondary Mortgage Market*". "[Our] entire housing finance system is not structured to meet the needs of that demographic," Dave believes. "If we were to simply replace Fannie Mae and Freddie Mac or recap and release, I think we would just get more of what we have now which is two companies that are not fulfilling the need of affordable housing."

The way forward and out, Stevens asserts, is a new system defined by "more competition." This approach, in Stevens' words "will force them to compete more effectively in the market and not play the duopoly game where they just simply manage a massive multi-trillion-dollar market between two entities ... that'll probably create natural tension to try to extend the markets into more communities." This, in turn, Stevens believes, will prevent the GSEs from leveraging their portfolios "as almost predatory instruments like they did pre-recession."

There is also real risk regarding the 2019 end of term of FHFA Director Melvin Watt. The FHFA (similar to the CFPB) uses a single appointed director structure, with the director having enormous power to impose the status quo or quantum change to the operational aspects of the GSEs. Unlike the CFPB, the director is subject to Senate confirmation. My own view is a comprehensive legislative solution is much preferred to the potential risks and vagaries of a replacement director appointment in the current caustic political environment.

GSE reform isn't coming any time soon, according to some I spoke with, including Patrick Sinks of MGIC, who believes that Congress won't act unless there is another crisis. Though the market works on a day to day basis, Sinks goes on, the private label market will not come back until there is certainty around GSEs reform.

Another maverick discussed the very slow change process at the GSEs and HUD. Barrett Burns noted:

[The credit scoring environment in the GSEs] requires originators to use '04 FICO models. '04 models FICO models were developed on data from 1995 to 2000 but think about that for a second... [it was] well before the recession. It's also back when things like paid collections were included in a scoring model. Things like rent and utilities were not included, so they're not as inclusive as they are today. The GSEs also use these credit scoring models for their pricing and for LLPA pricing. The mortgage insurance companies are forced to use the FICO credit scoring models for their pricing... For a new credit scoring model to be in place, it's really pretty amazing how many organizations have to be in line... mortgage insurers. Investors. People who create prepayment models. It is really complex, very complicated. And it shouldn't be. You know, when credit card lenders or auto finance lenders switch models, it's a pretty easy process for them, they're used to doing it... investors and fixed income investors on the mortgage side and all the users all the way through...aren't used to changing credit scoring models. So, it's a simple solution to broadening credit, but exceptionally difficult operationally to pull it off.

I asked Barrett if he felt the industry was missing out on a pretty big opportunity to serve additional borrowers. His response was as follows:

Well we did a study. Because the FHA kept saying, "well, it's too costly to accommodate you guys." Our pitch has been allowing lenders to use either FICO or us, and they'd only be looking at the expense side of it. So, we did some modeling on that...With consumers with a 620 and above, we score about 7.6 million more people than our competitor does. So, then we stripped out anybody who had a foreclosure. Anybody who owns a home. Anybody who has a 90-day past due. Anybody under 25. Anybody over 70. It came down to—depending on different interest rates—anywhere between 2.6 million to 2.8 million. Just because of a credit score alone.

An in-depth conversation with Stan Middleman led to some very different ideas with regards to credit availability. Mr. Middleman stated:

Some people shouldn't be homeowners. So, if people who should be renters are prohibited from being homeowners, I think you're doing them a favor." In characteristically blunt language, Stan also asserted that the idea that regulation (or "over-regulation") has restricted access is "nonsense."

Mr. Middleman, looking backwards, noted that restricting access to credit as the only viable answer for an industry considering the bottom line [when reflecting back on the 2004-2008 subprime period]:

We have a rule here when we make a loan—No matter what we're going to do with that loan, we expect to be paid back. And I'm not sure that people think people have to pay loans back. In lending terms [the old subprime segment of the industry was] much more liberal than the FHA. That would indicate to me that [the subprime segment of the industry] is not expecting to get paid back. One out of every five borrowers [defaulted]. And I know

I can't run a business that's for profit under those conditions. If we were a not for profit, then maybe that would be a fine set of circumstances [under which] four out of five borrowers pay it back ... supporting the one that doesn't, well, that's a societal decision... But if you're going to run for-profit businesses and you're going to lend money [like a subprime lender], you have to have the fundamental rule going in that the customer has to be able to pay you back or you have to be able to have enough collateral. That can replace the customer's predilection to pay back.

It should be noted that Mr. Middleman's Freedom Mortgage is a major lender in FHA, VA, and GSE conventional lending across the credit spectrum, serving thousands of low to moderate income borrowers that meet current respective FHA, VA, and GSE credit standards.

It's important to understand the construct of credit scoring models. According to materials provided by Barrett Burns of VantageScore:

The scoring process begins with a sample of consumer credit files at the beginning and end of a two-year performance window. Through a process called logistic regression, modelers determine the credit attributes at the beginning of the window that were predictive of actual performance over the following two years. These attributes form the model algorithm. Next, they apply the resulting algorithm to rank order consumers based on their probability of default (PD), where default is typically defined as missing a payment on any obligation by 90 days or more.

The three-digit credit score is only a representation of rank order: rather than have 220 million people, each with his or her own individual ranking (i.e., 1 to 220 million!), credit score models compress the consumer ranks into twenty-point bands.

For models that perform well, that rank order will hold across the economic cycle such that a score of 600 always suggests a higher level of risk than a 700 and a lower level than a 500. The specific PD at each of those scores, however, will change with the overall economy.

This is the source of common and widespread misunderstanding. The relationship between a credit score and PD is dynamic: it is defined at the time the model is initially developed but changes over time as the overall risk level in the economy ebbs and flows. The rank order, however, is stable over time.

My view is the lookback over consumer behaviors modeled by a credit score is much more valuable than a point-in-time look at income. The exclusion of income from credit scoring and the dynamic nature of scoring models also make them valuable for performance monitoring of loans over time. No need to recompute income to monitor a servicing portfolio.

As the industry begins to have a conversation around expanding access to credit, it will need to find a balancing point between these two points of view. The industry cannot ignore the fact that FHA delinquencies are currently 9.8% and serious delinquencies are 1.8%.[22] Ignoring the needs of the marketplace will not pan out for the mortgage industry in the long term, but neither will ignoring the

---

[22] MBA Delinquency Survey, Third Quarter 2017.

dangers. National policy has focused on increasing the homeowner-ship rate since the late 1980s. The subprime meltdown of 2007-2010 clarified the downside of making credit standards too flexible. That lesson has been learned. Congressional action via Dodd-Frank, the CFPB, and a plethora of private litigation has driven the pendulum to the other extreme—that being a restrictive credit box—and constrained availability of credit to borrowers who do not fit neatly into the Qualified Mortgage ("QM") definition.

The QM and Ability to Repay requirements are mechanistic and impose a one-size-fits-all approach to credit. In some cases, the 43% maximum debt ratio is too restrictive for some borrowers. In other cases, 43% may be too much for some borrowers. Nonetheless, the carve out for higher ratios that "fit" the GSE AUS standards distorts the market for private credit. Private credit is subject to the 43% limit. There are efforts between the industry, legislators, and regulators to consider these points, but significant progress in the current toxic political environment is not likely.

So how does one reconcile differing views regarding access to credit? I've done substantial research into the factors that drive loan performance. First, borrower past behavior managing financial matters is the single most important factor for evaluating prospective loan performance. Responsible behavior in paying obligations is foundational for FICO scoring. But FICO scores do not consider some of the scorable behaviors of applicants that VantageScore considers. Patty Arvielo notes that she has observed cultural factors where family and friends assist a borrower in making payments, and this cannot be readily scored by the current FICO scoring standard.

Second, down payment—or "skin in the game"—is the close second in predicting loan performance. Skin in the game, whether the borrower's or a private mortgage insurer's, protects the investor if a borrower cannot pay.

Income, according to a Federal Reserve study discussed in depth below, is not a significant predictor of loan performance; yet Congress has hard-coded debt to equity into the Ability to Repay rules. Income, unlike credit score and equity, is a "point in time" snapshot. Most employees in the U.S. are at-will. This means they can be terminated for cause or no cause anytime by the employer. Similarly, the employee can quit at any time, for any reason. Yet the industry insists on an extraordinarily complicated computation of income for qualification purposes. The Fannie Mae Guide devotes over 200 pages of technical discussion to the computation and use of income in qualification. Income that could end tomorrow if the borrower loses their at-will job. But get it wrong, and you'll repurchase the loan.

I learned early in my career that poor credit habits were not confined to any income group. As a young lender I was amazed to discover some doctors, lawyers, TV personalities, and professional athletes had very poor credit scores. Why? Despite high income, some were careless and didn't pay obligations on time. Some lived beyond their means. Some had substance abuse issues. The list goes on. I was equally amazed that applicants of modest income had very good credit scores, even those who on paper appeared to have very high debt-to-income ratios.

I also learned that borrower explanations of credit blemishes ("cry letters") could also be useful in making underwriting judgements. Some letters were obviously coached, but others rang true. The most moving was a 1991 letter that began, "My bad credit issues started in the backseat of a Buick on a beautiful starlit night..."

and told the story of how this applicant had gotten her life back on track, how she had paid off her arrearages and needed a chance to buy a first home for her and her 4-year-old daughter. This was an authentic letter of explanation from the heart. We made the loan and it performed.

As an industry, we've lost the ability to apply human judgement and compassion in the name of Ability to Repay regulations and fair lending concerns. Nonetheless, a more commonsense approach to broadening scoring engine results and a less mechanistic approach to income and debt-to-income ratios could go a long way to easing access to credit to non-traditional borrowers.

More Valuable Metrics

My early days in mortgage banking in the late 1980s were spent working for John DePatto, a long-time lender and bank executive. John and I discussed the relative importance of income computation and documentation. John was a pretty colorful character, and told me, "Borrower behavior is a far more important metric than income. Most employees are at-will and can be fired anytime. Yet we chase the borrower to document his or her income." John continued, "Behavior can be seen by analyzing the credit report and how well the borrower meets obligations. A borrower paying as agreed means that the behaviors of living within one's means, having a nest egg, and protecting their credit history are ingrained in their conduct of their financial lives." It made sense.

He showed me a loan file of a highly compensated executive whose debt-to-income ratio was modest, but whose file was riddled with delinquencies. On paper, he could afford the loan. In practice, this high-public profile individual was reported to have substance abuse issues. Spending on illegal substances doesn't appear on a credit report or the 1008 loan application. Prior delinquency was offset by the mitigating factor of low debt-to-income ratio. The loan went through foreclosure.

FICO credit scores are highly predictive of loan performance for scored borrowers and *do not* include income as an element of the model. FICO scores are so important that a prospective borrower who does not have a credit score may have more difficulty accessing the mortgage marketplace. "No Score" applicants are often first-time home buyers, members of a minority as classified by the Government Monitoring Information on an application, an immigrant, or all of the above.

Later in my career, I had the opportunity to formally research the impact of income on loan performance. The research conclusions were not surprising to me: Income is not a primary predictor of loan performance, as reported by the Federal Reserve. Ability to Repay has codified the income element of debt-to-income ratio as a hurdle that hits first-time, minority, non-traditional and immigrant applicants very hard, even though it is not a primary indicator of loan performance.

If change needs to happen, and if stable income is an inexact or even unfair metric to use in today's economy, what metrics should the industry objectively rely on? According to "Credit Risk, Credit Scoring, and the Performance of Home Mortgages" published by the Federal Reserve Board's Division of Research and Statistics[23], credit score and loan-to-value ratios are much more valuable metrics.

[23] Robert B. Avery et al., "Credit Risk, Credit Scoring, and the Performance of Home Mortgages," Federal Reserve Bulletin, vol. 82 no. 7 (1996).

What the data showed, the report said, was that the relationship between borrower income and loan performance was "slight" at best. In the document, the Fed stated that, "Most models of mortgage loan performance emphasize the role of the borrower's equity in the home in the decision to default. So long as the market value of the home (after accounting for sales expenses and related costs) exceeds the market value of the mortgage, the borrower has a financial incentive to sell the property to extract the equity rather than default."[24] The Fed further stated that, "Delinquencies, particularly serious ones, are often resolved when the borrower sells the property and uses the proceeds to pay off the loan."[25]

Of course, few observers expected home prices to decline in 2006-2010 as severely as they did. The decline in home value resulted in many loans being underwater, with the value of the home less than the amount of the mortgage. Underwater mortgages resulted in strategic defaults through which a borrower could pay but wouldn't pay. Strategic defaults cannot be easily modeled, as many underwater mortgages continued to perform, and many did not... without any apparent observable factual indicators to show the propensity of a borrower to pay when the loan was underwater, or to send in the keys. It comes down to a borrower's character and whether the borrower views the mortgage as a contract or as "project finance" with an option where one can walk away on economics alone. It also highlights the adverse impact of judicial foreclosure processes, where a borrower simply playing the system could stay in a home two, three or more years without making a payment.

---

[24] Robert B. Avery et al., "Credit Risk, Credit Scoring, and the Performance of Home Mortgages," *Federal Reserve Bulletin*, vol. 82 no. 7 (1996), pp. 622-623
[25] Ibid, p. 622.

Furthermore, the Fed reported that the data showed that, "…[S]urprisingly, after controlling for other factors, the initial ratio of debt payment to income has been found to be, at best, only weakly related to the likelihood of default.[26] … Foreclosure rates are substantially higher for borrowers with low credit scores as well as for those with high loan-to-value ratios . . . Credit score and, to a lesser extent, loan-to-value ratio appears to be much stronger predictors of foreclosure rates than income." Yet, "Ability to Repay" requirements are hardcoded into regulation.

What's more, the Fed report found that loan performance parsed by credit score or loan-to-value ratio transcended income; in other words, performance patterns gauged by credit score or loan-to-value ratio "are very similar for borrowers at all income levels."[27]

These statistical observations are in keeping with the thinking of Patrick Sinks of MGIC on the issue of the credit risk management used by private mortgage insurers, particularly the role of credit score and down payment on typical customers needing private mortgage insurance because of having only a 5 or 10% down payment. Not just in the GSE private mortgage insurance, but also the private label and non-QM space. Patrick observed:

> I think it has to be a collective effort… there's a lot of debate about housing goals, GSE housing goals, and does that cause bad behavior. On the other hand, obviously it's kind of 'motherhood' and 'apple pie'. People think "Well, that's a good thing. Let's try to get more people in homes and let's keep them in homes." So that's why I say it has to be

---

[26] Ibid, p. 624

[27] Avery et al., Credit Risk, Credit Scoring, pp. 633-635.

a collective effort, whether it's agency lending or – to your point—private label where people are going to say, "you know we're really going to stand up as partners" … everybody involved in the origination process—the lender, the MI company, the appraisal company, all that are involved in the process. It has to be a collective effort. I think there has to be a better understanding about the layering of risk. Clearly one of the lessons that came out of the Great Recession was you know the layering of risk—high LTV high DTI, low credit score —and it just blew up. We just can't go down that path again… you can't set a goal for the sake of setting a goal. In the case of the agencies, they're forced to pick a number or a percentage of their income… [On] the private label side you can say realistically "what can we do here" as opposed to setting some audacious goal and saying, "OK now come hell or high water we got to hit it." So, I think, number one, it takes a collective effort. Number two, I think it takes a greater understanding, a common understanding, among the parties as to what the risks are in the layering of risk and what that could mean. You know, one of the concerns now, from a credit side— and it could affect even a business or affect views on more affordable housing—and that is the rise in house prices and what that means now… that is what I mean by the impact on markets. Obviously, if you're in an affordable housing space you try to get more people in homes, but prices are rising. And if there's some kind of recession at some point in time—even a mild recession, which we would hope it would be—then house prices and the drop-in home prices would clearly impact the entire market, there is a ripple effect. So, I think we got to watch that as well.

Fair Isaac & Company ("FICO") describes itself as "the leading provider of independent third-party credit scores. Founded in 1956, FICO introduced analytic solutions such as credit scoring that have made credit more widely available, not just in the United States but around the world. FICO pioneered the development and application of critical technologies behind decision management. These include predictive analytics, business rules management and optimization. FICO uses these technologies to help businesses improve the precision, consistency and agility of their complex, high–volume decisions. Many FICO products reach industry-wide adoption — such as the FICO® Score, the standard measure of consumer credit risk in the United States."[28]

FICO scores use five elements to estimate the probability of default by a borrower:

- Payment history

- Amount owed

- Length of credit history

- Types of credit in use

- New credit

FICO also specifies information it does ***not*** use in computing a FICO score. FICO does not use "salary, occupation, title, employer, date employed or employment history" or "any information *that is not proven to be predictive of future credit performance* [emphasis

---

[28] FICO, ABOUT US | FICOTM, http://www.fico.com/en/about-us#at_glance, June 25, 2015.

added]". So, FICO suggests income data is not material to loan performance… but ATR codifies it as a federal requirement under Dodd-Frank[29].

A New Approach

So, what if the traditional FICO score doesn't express the appropriate degree of odds of repayment for non-traditional borrowers discussed above? According to VantageScore, a venture created in 2005 by the three major credit repositories, "using a broader and deeper set of credit file data and more advanced modeling techniques, the VantageScore model can provide credit scores for 30-35 million consumers who are invisible to legacy credit scoring models." That's a group of prospects larger than the population of Texas, if you can imagine.

"Roughly 10 million of those consumers have scores of 600 or higher, which makes them attractive prospects to many lenders. Approximately 9.7 million of the consumers who are newly scorable with VantageScore are African-American or Hispanic, and about 2.7 million of them have scores of 600 or higher."

Barrett Burns of VantageScore stated that the Federal Housing Finance Agency's recently released Annual Housing Report indicated that only $322 million purchased by the GSEs were score-less mortgages in 2016. This is in contrast to $976 billion of unpaid principal balances.

---

[29] There may be instances when knowledge or estimates of future income prospects may be material to loan performance, in the case of a newly graduating doctor or other licensed professional.

Mr. Burns told me in our discussions that he is optimistic about the viability of opening up credit standards. "Our belief is by using more and newer models that use better architecture, and so forth, greatly expands the scorable universe without reducing standards." It would take a good deal of lifting and cohesion across the mortgage industry, however. "It's really pretty amazing how many organizations need to be in line: mortgage insurers, investors, people who create prepayment models... it's really complex." As per usual, things are simpler in other industries. "When credit card lenders or auto finance lenders switch models, it's a pretty easy process for them." In the mortgage industry, he says, broadening credit is a "simple solution, but incredibly difficult."

By Mr. Burns calculations, sticking with the old standards is alienating as many as 2.8 million households. One jarring fact is that a third of these households are Black and Latino. Moving forward, as national demographics continue to shift dramatically, can the mortgage industry continue to ignore the needs of this market sector?

Patty and Rick Arvielo stress that any in-roads into minority homebuying communities need to focus on culture, not ethnicity. This is the kind of high-touch topic that betrays the weakness in automation. As the Arvielos frame it, we need to underwrite to culture and "you can't automate that." While addressing minority needs is now an industry-wide conversation, however, the industry is still not ready for it. As Bill Cosgrove put it, the industry talks out of both sides of its mouth on this issue. While we all know that minority ownership is not where it should be, he told me, many of the rules are still lined up against those loans falling into place.

Phil DeFronzo recalls many situations where a "make-sense" loan cannot be done within a GSE context: a divorcee with 60% cash down payment from a divorce settlement, but no income currently; a doctor with a contract in hand from a hospital but hasn't started working yet; the list goes on.

Jamie Korus-Pearce, Nathan Burch, and others recall many instances of borrowers that don't meet the specific technical requirements of an investor but nonetheless appear willing and able to repay the loan as agreed. According to Nathan, "Underwriting judgment has been eliminated by regulations and punitive enforcement." Jamie recalls when it was possible to grant "common sense" underwriting decisions based on the judgment of a skilled underwriter. "No more", unfortunately.

One thing is clear from all this: the industry, Congress, HUD, federal and state regulators, Freddie Mac and Fannie Mae need to quickly re-visit underwriting and documentation criteria, with an end goal of ensuring that the criteria are appropriately evaluating the credit risk of both traditional and non-traditional borrowers. The current regulatory climate has a very real cost in terms of access to credit and the economic cost of regulations. Rethinking responsible regulation, GSE reform and common-sense approaches to credit access require the good-faith efforts of the industry, legislators and regulators.

The time is now.

CHAPTER THREE
Business Process and Workflow Strategies of the Maverick CEO

The Loan Manufacturing Process: Why Do Costs Keep Rising?

As I began researching this book, one startling fact kept coming back to me again and again: a major car manufacturer such as General Motors spends about $2,300 in labor to build a car. In marked contrast, the mortgage industry spends about $2,600[30] in operational labor to document a loan. The total cost to close one mortgage loan is a whopping $8,800[31].

The more one thinks about the detail in this, the more jarring it becomes. A car consists of more than 30,000 parts from the smallest screw to the engine block and frame, and it runs (at least for now) off internal combustion. A mortgage, in short, is a stack of documents. How can we as an industry explain the fact that building a mortgage file is more complex or more labor-intensive than a car?

---

[30] MBA Mortgage Banking Performance Data, First Quarter 2017 data as computed by the author.
[31] Ibid.

We often talk about the "loan manufacturing process" in the industry. If it is, then, a manufacturing process, why is it so labor intensive and disorganized? What are the steps we need to take as an industry to streamline processes? Are there technologies in place that can aid in this?

During my time as a lender, I helped Jamie Flinchbaugh, an acquaintance who is an authority on Lean Manufacturing, obtain a mortgage. Jamie is a Contributing Editor for Industry Week magazine and holds Master of Science in Mechanical Engineering degrees from the Massachusetts Institute of Technology and the University of Michigan, as well as a Mechanical Engineering degree from Lehigh University.

I learned from Jamie that lean manufacturing principles seek to maximize value while minimizing the cost of providing that value. "Value" is any action or process that a customer would be willing to pay for. Lean looks carefully at the back-end processes for creating value. Minimizing cost through lean manufacturing is a systematic method for waste minimization within a manufacturing system without sacrificing productivity.

Lean also considers waste created through "overburden", such as employees working in processes where they are not fully trained, poorly laid-out workflows, unclear instructions, a lack of proper tools to perform the required work, unreliable processes, and poor communication.

Another form of waste is created by unevenness in workloads, which can cause inefficiency. According to Jamie, lean manufacturing makes obvious what adds value, by seeking to reduce anything and everything that is not adding value.

Like my daughter Christina, Jamie had many comments on the lending process. His central theme was, "how can a lender make a straightforward process so unnecessarily complex and filled with what appears to be so many non-value adding activities"?

We spoke about the lending process, focusing on assessing the likelihood of repayment of a loan. In Jamie's mind, correctly assessing the likelihood of repayment added the most value to the mortgage process. We discussed Fannie Mae's "Comprehensive Credit Assessment" protocol. FNMA stated that two primary factors indicate the likelihood of repayment of a mortgage: the equity investment (down payment) paid by the borrower and the credit history for all the borrowers who are applying for the mortgage. Low down payment and low credit score are the Primary Risks decreasing the likelihood of repayment. Significant down payment and high credit score increases the likelihood of repayment.

FNMA described Contributory Risk factors as those risk factors that are not of sufficient weight by themselves for a lender to use as the basis for reaching an underwriting decision. However, depending on the level of Primary Risk factors or other Contributory Risk factors, the FNMA protocol suggested that Contributory Risk factors may influence the default risk of the mortgage. [An extended discussion of Fannie Mae's Comprehensive Risk Assessment occurs later in this book. Fannie Mae automated the Comprehensive Risk Assessment in its Desktop Underwriting ("DU") Automated Underwriting System ("AUS").]

Jamie's conclusion was, "Loan decisions shouldn't be that hard, since they are based on objective data with criteria that can be evaluated by an AUS algorithm. Lean should be easy to apply."

Borrower versus Loan Investor

This led me to the thought that the borrower focuses on two principal dimensions: the cost of the loan, and how fast it can be completed. The investor focuses on the likelihood of repayment. The needs of the borrower and investor are not in alignment—the borrower wants the lowest cost, fastest loan, and the investor wants a loan with a high likelihood of repayment, with a risk adjusted return to compensate the investor for the risk the lender is taking. The regulators add the third dimension: 700 pages to prove that all requirements have been documented and the borrower has disclosures that completely detail loan terms.

The borrower wants a friendly loan officer and/or digital process that makes the process as easy as possible. The loan officer works primarily on building a relationship and securing the sale. As Nathan Burch put it, the loan officer is the "quarterback of the loan. He or she starts the process in motion according to their game plan."

Depending on the loan officer, there is great variation in the quality of the data obtained by the loan officer during the loan application process. Data quality translates into data integrity to the investor: the data provided by the borrower and from other sources must be accurate, complete and current. I've asked many loan officers "who is your customer?" The answer is usually, "the borrower." If the loan is a purchase transaction, the loan officer usually adds the realtor as a customer. The loan officer adds the realtor because "I'm only as good as my last deal, and the realtor won't recommend me if I don't deliver."

Interestingly, I've *never* been told by a loan officer that the end investor is the customer, even though the end investor must buy the loan product that the Loan Officer is selling. No end investor, no loan closing for secondary market, no salable loans and no commission.

Martin Kerr, the President of Bestborn Business Solutions (developers of Loan Vision, a loan level mortgage accounting platform), shed clarity on why Lean isn't easy to apply to mortgage banking. There are really two customers on each mortgage banking transaction: the borrower of the money, and the investor purchasing the loan. According to Martin, most retail mortgage banking operations are headed by executives primarily with a sales background in generating loan applications from consumers. The focus of these sales-led organizations is primarily the borrowers. The operational side of the business must deal with the "other" customer—the investor.

That is why it is so important to start with the back end operational processes where the customer served is the mortgage investor. Getting the requirements of the investor hard coded into the operational process and workflow as the end goal then lets the process and workflow correctly assemble needed information from the borrower. That makes the process from Initial Interest to Application much more likely to *gather and document required information properly the first time,* and minimize or eliminate rework or new requests for information to the borrower.

Martin explained:

> *"My views come from my background because I was in manufacturing and was a process engineer. It was all about doing things efficiently and getting an understanding of every single step of what you do has to be there. And then the keyword is what you would call 'constraints'. You have*

a constraint somewhere which slows everything down, and so on. Which seems like common sense.

Many mortgage banks have been started by salespeople, right? They were successful LOs who have ended up as entrepreneurs. And the whole organization is set up to keep the sales people happy. When it comes to what mortgage bankers do, they're a manufacturer. They make the loans.

Remember, if you have a problem at the beginning of the process then that problem flows all the way down. So, it causes knock-on effects all the way down the process. It absolutely must add pain to underwriting, and absolutely must add pain in processing the loan because the focus is very sales orientated. The sales people don't care about process downstream.

From a technology standpoint and from an effort standpoint CEOs will remove bottlenecks through the sales process. They will absolutely invest in CRM technology or lead generation technology and making it easier when a loan officer is working with borrower. But once that came the application is taken, everyone else will deal with it downstream. And at that first point of contact, if that data wasn't managed as well as it could be; (the rest is confusion)."

We will discuss this in greater detail at various points through the book, but it is important to address this central issue for a moment—the borrower's desire for high touch in mortgage banking when needed. As we have all these conversations about digitally transforming the industry, we will need to return again and again to this question—how can we maintain a high touch, customer-friendly approach while adapting to the new tech environs of the 21st century?

Internal Operations at Lenders

The trouble with loan manufacturing for traditional retail lenders starts right at the beginning. The overarching desire at most lenders today is to recruit, accommodate, and retain high producers. As such, the lending process for retail operations can easily be defined as "loan officer centric". Generally speaking, these loan officers tend to be extremely independent and want to do business their way. Lenders, in keeping with this, tend to be accommodating of loan officer demands.

While keeping high producers happy has its benefits, in the gestalt this approach prevents lenders (and, as an extension, the industry) from creating a *tightly defined* loan process from inception. Each loan is beholden to the individual processes and work practices of the loan officer and how he or she "does business." Jonathan Corr at Ellie Mae addressed this rather colorfully, describing it as filling process holes and leaks with human spackle when automation and reengineering are more direct and efficient answers.

Tim Nguyen of BeSmartee articulated the issue with retail originators. According to Tim:

> *What many in the industry see is that good originators are very difficult to come by. There's a limited number of them. That's a big problem that's very prevalent in traditional retail. There's such a small supply of quality originators who can actually produce business. And there is a big demand for Originators and with big demand you have companies chasing these originators down. Better comp. Better employee incentive programs. Better facilities, better tools. You rely on these originators to produce revenue. You're going to get caught in that game.*

If you look at Consumer Direct, the MBA data shows the profitability per loan officer and the production per loan officer is much higher. I believe the number is about two to three times more productivity comes from a consumer direct loan officer than the traditional retail loan officer.

That makes sense because the company is paying for marketing cost, call center costs, branding costs and advertising. The company is picking up those bills. So, they need consumer direct loan officers to be more productive. They need to pay them less per loan since the scope of that originator is lead conversion and technical skill to be able to get that loan done quickly.

Fortunately, technology and its advocates are starting to step in to offer some automation and streamlining for loan officers. Consumer applications and data gathering have experienced a leap forward with services such as BeSmartee, Blend, and Roostify, to name just a few. On the loan officer side, LO-oriented tools such as SimpleNexus and Maxwell allow LOs to reduce the back and forth tediousness of manual processing and close loans sooner and more efficiently. A mobile application transitions the process away from paper-based transactions, features push notifications for quick action when needed, and generally makes both the LO's and the borrower's life easier.

Direct to consumer lending can have a much more defined process, with controls over the customer experience and process. Quicken has a *very* defined process for direct to consumer. Any lender that has broad flexibility with retail loan officers can have a tightly defined consumer direct process.

Wholesale lending in some ways is more complex than retail lending. Brokers tend to focus on getting the loan done, and many do not have the technology sophistication of larger lenders. There seems to be more diversity in practice with wholesale lenders, particularly multi-channel (retail, direct to consumer, wholesale, and correspondent) lenders. The more defined and integrated the wholesale lending process is, the better the customer experience, where the broker is considered the actual customer.

I've spoken to many brokers over my career, and one theme is say "no" quickly to a loan if it doesn't fit. Same for the broker's process that doesn't fit the lender. But if the lender is highly automated and the broker has difficulty transmitting a DU3.2 file, it's probably not a good match. The broker will need much personal interaction.

Really, automation of the documentation process cannot happen soon enough. In fact, the back and forth is one of the main factors in the loan manufacturing cycle slowing things down. As anyone who has been on either side of the mortgage process knows, few files are complete at application, resulting in many round-trips for information to be updated or corrected during the process. This greatly increases costs, consumer dissatisfaction, and time from application to closing.

It's not the prettiest of pictures and would certainly set off anyone with even the most marginal knowledge of process efficiency. Remember the mortgage banking process diagram from the first chapter? Now add the re-touches and rework that may be required during the loan process. I've measured the number of touches and retouches in a loan process in many lenders, and it's high. The MBA statistics suggest that the typical loan takes 40-60 hours on operational and support labor. MBA data suggests underwriter productivity is about two loans a day. An underwriter's all-in compensation cost easily exceeds $100,000 per annum in major metro areas. This suggests it costs over $200 per file for just underwriting direct labor. Thank goodness, DU and LP are "free".

It bears mentioning at this point that the typical manufacturing process does not look anything like the lending process diagramed in the first chapter. In fact, typical manufacturing operations tend to have a one-way flow without rework, especially in the post Lean Six Sigma days of process optimization. One insightful observation about this came from Bill Emerson. He told me that there needs to be a new focus on integrating data instead of collecting pieces of paper. This conceptual shift seems key to me, and the ideal way to integrate the front and back ends of the process to create a seamless whole.

Of course, as David Motley put it, the mortgage manufacturing process is mired down by the "raw materials" coming in. When he and I discussed the jarring statistic of how many labor hours go into a car vs. a mortgage, he cannily observed that a car is built with consistent materials and with the same endgame (meaning one can "begin with the end in mind" every time). On the other hand, each mortgage (especially the traditional retail and broker channels) has a set of "raw materials" that are sometimes as different from one another as each person asking for a mortgage is. Automation needs to find a way to systematize these widely varied raw materials throughout the process.

How efficiently this manufacturing process works varies across the industry. The picture is brighter with direct to consumer loans. Direct to consumer loan officers are dependent upon their lender for leads. The direct to consumer process tends to be more defined and more automated from the start. That being said, there are still round trips between functions due to incomplete or erroneous data.

Wholesale operations on the other hand are broker-centric, with an overarching desire to recruit, accommodate and retain high producing brokers. As discussed, brokers are independent and are motivated by the best compensation and the best operational process. Many brokers tend to want lenders to adopt to the broker's business model. There are many round trips between functions due to incomplete or erroneous data, and some brokers' origination systems do not directly interface into the lender's systems, creating data transfer and data integrity issues.

Correspondent-lending operations are correspondent-centric, with a desire to recruit, accommodate, and retain high-producing correspondent lenders. Because correspondents lend their own money and must have the loan purchased in a short time period, correspondent lenders tend to be compliant with aggregating correspondent lenders' systems.

What we can glean from all of these, however, is that data integrity is critical—mission critical. Weakness in the data integrity link is the reason for these round trips; ensuring data integrity is the surest way to ensure a streamlined manufacturing process for a loan. In this way, we can create the consistency of "raw materials" that we need to create a truly efficient mortgage manufacturing process.

Addressing the Cost of Regulation

There cannot be any conversation around controlling costs in the mortgage industry without a detailed investigation of regulatory cost. According to the Competitive Enterprise Institute's annual survey, the federal regulatory cost reached $1.885 trillion in 2015. This translates into a whopping $15,000 per household in federal regulations.

This, of course, is not just a legislative issue, but a federal agency issue. As an example, the CEI survey delivers some compelling detail on agency regulation as relates to federal mandate. In 2015, while Congress enacted 114 laws, agencies responded by creating over 3,400 rules, an impressive 30 rules per law.

That's a lot of red tape. And a lot of money.

Across the US economy, according to the CEI, compliance costs have now outpaced individual *and* corporate income tax to the tune of $1.82 trillion. Phil DeFronzo, the CEO and founder of Norcom Mortgage, discussed with me the burden regulations have placed on IMBs. "There's a lot of overlap and duplication in regulations and audits. If you look at somebody like us who's an independent mortgage banker that has to be licensed in various states, I think so far, this year we've had six audits. From different states. There's duplication of so many regulations... a great percentage of what we do now is just regulatory overkill... It's been a real big [reason for] increasing cost for a lender our size."

For Jonathan Corr, the time to act effectively is now. People aren't running around "with their hair on fire" when it comes to regulation, so there's no better time to take a holistic approach to compliance. For Nima Ghamsari, the regulatory environment was a key factor in slowing down the adoption of new technologies the mortgage industry needs to get ahead. According to Nima, between 2012 and 2015, lenders were 100% focused on regulatory compliance and weren't thinking about innovation as much as a result. That is different now: "I think adoption is [becoming] extremely accelerated." Clearly, adoption at the point of "Consumer Interest to Application" is speeding up quickly. But Tim Nguyen sees existing regulation as one of the central stumbling blocks to a "one-click" close. From whichever perspective one comes, it is clear that there is consensus that regulations must be addressed in order to enable end-to-end innovation in mortgage lending.

Process and Workflow

The process used by a lender involves moving from the very beginning of the customer's interest in your company all the way through taking the application to closing the loan, establishing the loan servicing experience, and serving that customer's financing needs for life.

Workflow is how the lender's process is translated into the order of the individual tasks necessary to complete the loan. Workflow extends to the lowest common denominator of each task within the process. Most lender's workflows appear to have a large amount of variability in what and how each task is to be accomplished. Most loan origination systems support milestones as a form of workflow management, but the tasks within each milestone are generally not planned and executed as they would be in a typical manufacturing operation.

Many CEOs think about mortgage lending as dividing between two segments. The first segment is Consumer Interest in a mortgage loan, through the completion of the Application Process. As shorthand, we'll call this "Interest to App". The second segment is the Application to Investor Funding, or "App to Fund".

CUSTOMER INITIAL INTEREST TO APPLICATION				APPLICATION TO CLOSING						
Shop	Compare	Pricing & Loan Types	Application & Disclosures	Processing	Underwriting	Prefunding QC	Closing	Post-Closing	Shipping & Condition Clearance	Funding

"Interest to App" is an exciting segment. It's where the prospective borrower shops, compares, and prices a loan. It's where most of the technology innovation has taken place to date. Whether it's Rocket Mortgage, Blend, BeSmartee, Roostify, Maxwell, SimpleNexus, or others – it's largely about transparency and ease of use for the customer.

In looking at the overall process, Jonathan Corr noted, "There's a lot of folks that are attacking the 'Interest to Application' segment, that front end of the process. It's exciting to see all the innovation and focus on that initial customer experience and leveraging technologies that are out there: Instant asset and deposit data; income verification. That's going to create a better experience for the consumer. But when we look at the overall mortgage origination process, that's but a fraction of the time and the cost and complexity that runs through a lender's operations."

Tim Nguyen, CEO of BeSmartee noticed the inefficiency of the mortgage banking business in the "Interest to App" space. According to Tim:

> *I got into the mortgage business by accident. I was hanging out with a buddy one day who was a real estate appraiser who said he needed to run off and do a job. He said you want to hang out and wait for me or you want to come with me. So, I said yeah, I'll come with you. He comes back, and he picks up a three-hundred-dollar check. And he introduced me to the real estate business. That's how I got started in the*

business. The reason why I stayed in this business is I did notice a lot of efficiencies. Very little innovation.

And I felt like it was going to be exciting to use technology to really change the game. And that's the reason why we're here to make things better, faster and cheaper for the consumer and for lenders as well. You know our goal is to really shift the paradigm and change the way people look at originating loans whether as a consumer or whether as a lender. Look at E-Trade who changed the game for self-service brokerage. Look at something like Wealthfront which is changing the way people invest money. Amazon. Expedia. All these models are out there. All these models disintermediate as many third parties as possible, bringing in as direct to the consumer as possible and using automation technology and big data to make it as quick clean and quality as possible. It's been there for years in many different industries. It just so happened that [the mortgage industry] is one of the last to really grab hold of it. And if you really look at history, technology has always been the game changer. Whether it's how we collected cotton, made the process more efficient with the cotton gin, it's always been technology making things easier faster and cheaper. And you know that is just natural."

So, the Interest to App segment seems pretty well served. But then that digital, efficient, and transparent world hits its analog equivalent – App to Funding. One CEO suggested App to Funding is where we throw mortgage banking back to the last century: largely manual processes that meander towards closing, followed by a crisis of "this loan has to close" and all hands jump on deck to make it so. And then repeat for the next loan.

Jonathan Corr noted, "As we go through the [App to Funding] process, invariably things change." The number of underwriting submissions and resubmissions, clear to close submissions, and pre-funding exceptions point to poorly implemented and/or poorly automated workflow. "Folks are trying to find out where those exceptions are rather than using technology to ferret out exceptions as the process goes along. You can think of that all the way through, so when we get into underwriting and coordinating the closing and the disclosures there is back and forth."

Rob Peterson, Chief Technology Officer at Teraverde®, noted, "We've used our technology to map the time it takes for each step in the lending process, and to count the number of resubmissions and rework on loan files. The variations in process, the number of times work is redone, can be astounding. The reason the operational elements of mortgage banking takes 50-70 hours of touch labor is related to regulation and secondary market documentation requirements, but it's also due to poor process and rework." Rob is an engineer trained in process and does not see the care in process design that he was used to in industrial engineering. "Process and workflow improvement is one of the biggest opportunities to reduce cost, increase profit and increase customer satisfaction".

Nima Ghamsari, CEO of Blend, sees a sometimes-inappropriate tradeoff between human labor and technology at many points within mortgage lending. "There are very high value roles in the mortgage process. The advice, the consumer, the education, the guidance, understanding different life events, understanding the consumers." In short, the relationship side of mortgage banking is one of the highest and best uses of human interaction. "Evaluating their credit especially for people who are outside the boxes. How do you understand somebody's credit? There's a lot of room for humans in this process but I don't think that the humans are being used effectively today. Over time the growth in technology will make a significant impact." The other side is having humans perform low value-added tasks, while paying salaries for processors, underwriters, closers, etc. One can argue this is inefficient, error-prone, and not customer-centric.

The Interest to App technology is well thought through and varies contextually as the customer and/or loan officer proceeds through shopping for a loan, pricing it, and making an application. Contextual means if the borrower selects "refinance", the technology takes the customer and/or the loan officer around all of the purchase questions. Think about TurboTax, and the contextual walk-through based on your personal tax situation.

After the application and initial data collection, many lenders' processes have great variability of what happens, when it happens, and fewer service level standards. Why? Martin Kerr, CEO of Loan Vision, suggests it's because most lending CEOs have their roots in origination, and that's where the emphasis is. In simpler times, pre-Dodd-Frank, that approach had fewer downsides. The cost of regulatory, disclosure, underwriting, and secondary market exceptions and the reputation risk that comes with these exceptions prompted many CEOs to throw bodies at the issue, and hire checkers who check checkers, etc.

Reputation risk is really worth careful consideration. Patrick Sinks of MGIC stated,

> *"I think part of the scars of the Great Recession are everybody's been sued. Everybody you know have had their names dragged across the newspapers and televisions. So those scars run deep, so they're paranoid. But one of the underreported*

stories of the Great Recession was the impact of the mortgage crisis in the boardrooms… mortgage businesses are humming along; record volumes were feeling good. You know the boards ought to feel good. All of a sudden it blows up and they're going 'Wait a minute, how does all this credit risk come back to me? Wait a minute, why are we getting sued?' And so, there is a visibility on the mortgage business at board levels that I don't think I've ever seen. And so, I think when you translate that into process, it's dot every I, cross every T, to an extreme."

Lenders could work on the App to Funding segment and can achieve great efficiencies. Jonathan Corr sees a similar picture. CEOs are "worried about buybacks on the compliance and regulatory side. They're worried about fines, about the CFPB coming in and putting me out of business… CEOs throw bodies at it. And that is what has increased the cost dramatically. Lenders have to fill the holes and the leaks with human spackle. Right. You know there's no reason to have all that human spackle and that cost and that inefficiency—that adds to the timeline."

"That's where I think there is tremendous opportunity," he continues. "You know we're working on our NextGen solution and we're going to increase workflow automation and data and intelligence to save vast amounts of cost and inefficiency. The beneficiary of that is going to be the consumer—closing a loan is going to take a lot less time, a lot less cost."

The Great Slowdown - The Inefficiency of Mortgage "Manufacturing"

Several CEOs candidly described their organizations' failures at creating a seamless, easy, intuitive and fast process. Several described adding front-end customer experience tools without re-engineering the whole lending process. The result was a workable, front-end experience from consumer interest to application. But from application through closing, the process often produced elements of the list from J.D. Power and other surveys of what damages the customer experience, and the customer relationship.

Why? I've looked at well over one hundred workflows from a variety of lenders. Very few of the workflows were designed from the back end forward. Few were designed *after* the introduction of TRID. Many processes simply had TRID (and all of the other regulatory and industry changes) superimposed on a process that may have its original design in the early to mid-2000's. As a result, there are many processes that are patched together, and checkers checking the checkers is a common solution to making a fundamentally ineffective process pass compliance and loan salability muster.

Jonathan Corr noted that the most successful use cases of the Encompass LOS occur when the lender assesses and optimizes their entire workflow from the back end forward *before* implementing Encompass. Otherwise, the lender is simply using a different technology to perform the same old process.

The TILA-RESPA Integrated Disclosure rules ("TRID")[32] up-ended the method of disclosure and increased penalties for errors in estimates. I've informally surveyed about 100 lenders and asked, "In advance of TRID, did the lender review their end-to-end process?" Not surprisingly, the typical answers were similar to, "The final TRID rule wasn't issued until just before the implementation date, after many delays. There was no time to think about end-to-end process, we were just trying to get TRID right". The result is pre-TRID processes working in a post-TRID world. The level of cures, as well as "checkers checking checkers" seems to be linked to the imposition of TRID and various other regulatory requirements in the origination process because the lender simply didn't have the time to re-think the overall lending process from the back end forward. There also appears to be a direct link in regulatory cost imposed post Dodd-Frank, with six operations employees for every four originators in 2016, compared to six originators for every four operations employees in 2009.

Some lenders speak of the "loan manufacturing process". This always intrigued me, since I didn't think of lending as a manufacturing process per se early in my career. So, I asked an accomplished CEO of a manufacturer of precision metal components to describe manufacturing to me.

---

[32] The industry is ripe with acronyms. My daughter's experience with lending acronyms came to a head when she reported to me an acronym I hadn't heard before – "YPS". Initially I though she meant "Yield Spread Premium" but was confused how she would know about that term, and it didn't apply to her transaction. She worked for a defense contractor and informed me that YPS means "Your Process Stinks" in relation to her mortgage experience with our industry. Christina is clearly influenced by her mother's candor.

What is Real Manufacturing?

Steve Shank, CEO of Flinchbaugh Engineering Inc. ("FEI") is a colleague and kindly provided background regarding the manufacturing process in the *actual* manufacturing world. FEI is a manufacturer of precision machined large and complex components, including industrial bearings, mining and earthmoving equipment transmission parts and large-scale compressor components to the energy industry. FEI serves many top industrial names that you would recognize, and it competes with US, European and Chinese competitors. Each part can run from hundreds to thousands of dollars when finished. In other words, Steve is someone who knows real manufacturing through and through.

Steve notes that "FEI manufactures parts with repeatable volume that are grouped and produced with similar parts we call "part families" using specifically optimized equipment we call "cells". This allows FEI to reduce variation, training costs and improve productivity."

The obvious analogy to lending is that "part families" are much like loan programs. Lenders sometimes specialize in a cell that focuses on a loan program group, such as FHA, etc. According to Steve,

> *FEI is not a 'job shop'. A job shop will commonly make a few parts for a prototype or a where a few units (usually less than a dozen) are needed. FEI is a medium scale production shop, enjoying the market, manufacturing between hundreds and thousands of parts within a part family. FEI is not a mass producer with complete automation (usually 10,000 parts or more).*

The first takeaway is that many lenders do operate as a job shop, where each loan is a prototype, and subject to the diversity of the loan officer, branch or loosely defined process and workflow of the lender. This "job shop" works for low volume purposes. It does not work for lenders closing 1,000 to 25,000 or more units per year.

We have learned that by grouping parts with common features or attributes, we are able to standardize and optimize change-overs (commonly called set-ups) and cycle time to maximize the number of parts produced within a given production run. We use an integrated business and workflow system, commonly called ERP or Enterprise Resource Planning, to plan, track and account for our performance.

We want everyone to know throughout the manufacturing process how they are performing versus an expected output and service levels. Everything and everyone is measured. We apply and incorporate Lean Manufacturing techniques throughout our process to eliminate wastes that are inherent to manufacturing... overproduction, waiting, transporting, unnecessary processing, unnecessary inventory, excess motion and defects.

We incentivize our operators to improve their processes and share that success through a larger profit-sharing check at the end of the year. We train our people to look for ways to improve productivity, reduce cost and impact our profitability. Our ability to remove these wastes effectively, results in all of our effort (and cost) being directed at creating value for our customers. When we do this well, and provide value without waste, we satisfy our customer's needs and our shareholders expectations."

Having walked FEI's manufacturing floor many times, I am amazed at how engaged the operators are in the process. There is attention to detail as a part progresses through as many as two hundred individual operations where manufacturing tolerances can be as little as 1/1000 of an inch—smaller than a human hair on parts that often weight hundreds or thousands of pounds. This manufacturing approach is nothing like most lending operations centers I have visited. Steve continues:

The operator will process the part on the assigned equipment. The process steps typically involve performing a machining operation on a lathe, mill, shaper, grinder and wash tank. In most cases, our operators will run two to three machines in a cellular environment.

When a good first piece is produced and the processes stable, we enter the production run phase. During the production run phase, the operator will perform in process checks and record performance to expected output. When expected output is not obtained, the team leader is engaged to problem solve as needed to improve output.

If expected output cannot be obtained, the operator and team leader record why for systematic problem solving. After the production run is completed, the final parts are then sampled for quality based on an inspection plan. After passing the sample inspection, the parts are transferred into finished goods and ready to ship to our customer.

As with any process, there is ample room for improvement. Much of our effort goes into doing an excellent job filtering opportunities up front, processing with well

trained and motivated operators, using the right equip-
ment and standard work instructions, reducing set-ups
and scrap, improving cycle-time and driving out all the
other waste.

And that, according to Steve, is how a world-class manufacturer operates. So, what can lenders learn from the process used by FEI (and many other world class manufacturers)?

The typical loan business process and workflow is unlike a standard manufacturing process in three ways:

- The loan process and workflow are not often truly standardized and are not well-documented. Actual practice diverges from the documented process.

- The loan process and workflow have multiple occasions where a loan file is sent back for re-work or correction.

- The loan process and workflow do not have detailed task level service levels that break down each element of process, and have a standard time, cost and sequence for that task.

Large variances occur in how long a process takes, the service levels associated with the process, and the standard cost of completing the process. The following chart first appeared in Chapter 1, but it is worth revisiting:

CREDIT METRICS	APPLICATION TO LOAN CLOSE DAYS	APPLICATION TO INVESTOR FUNDING DAYS
FICO < 640; LTV> 90%, DTI > 40%	43	61
FICO >740; LTV< 70%, DTI < 31%	42	60
All other loans	43	61
Lender Average	42	61
Standard Deviation	19	20

A standardized manufacturing process would have little variation. Loans vary in complexity based on loan purpose, borrower's sources of income, down payment and loan product. Perhaps each major segment of loan characteristics would have its own tight distribution. For example, one would expect high credit score, low LTV, and low DTI loans to move quickly though the system. Conversely one would expect lower credit score, higher LTV, and higher DTI to take longer. Alas, live data (anonymized) for actual lenders proves differently. Said another way, the statistics above indicate all loans, regardless of risk characteristic, transit through the lender's system in one manner: slowly and expensively.

We'll discuss how a lender might re-envision their lending process later in the book. For now, let's look at those who have excelled in customer satisfaction, despite the complexities holding back the industry.

High Performing Lenders

Relationships can be leveraged by technology. While there are a few still out there who believe technology gets in the way, it's safe to say digital can mean more engagement and more satisfaction. This is proven by a lender that never meets its customers face to face but has earned the highest satisfaction rating for loan origination eight years in a row—Quicken Loans.

How did they do it? Well, Bill Emerson and his team were definitely mavericks in 1998, and they took risks that could just as easily have played out very differently. As Bill tells it, Dan Gilbert, owner of Quicken Loans, started the conversation by sending out an email telling the team that they were "behind the eight ball". The internet was the way to go, he said. What would become RocketMortage was born. Perhaps most startling is the fact that the site was practically plug-and-play for the consumer, back in 1999. "You could literally have your credit pulled and lock in an interest rate," as Dan Gilbert described it, highlighting that such ease of use is only *just* becoming mainstream today.

After this intrepid start, Quicken would go on to become an industry leader and innovator. How? As Bill Emerson states, one needs to really consider the entire process from loan servicing, securitization, and then forward to customer experience. If the process is not *engineered* from the back-end forward, so much initial favorable customer satisfaction can be lost post application. It's no surprise then that Quicken also has the best loan servicing customer satisfaction four years running as of this writing. It's also no surprise that one of Quicken's slogans is "Engineered to Amaze".

It's interesting to compare Quicken with its nearest competitor in the 2015 J.D. Power survey, Fifth Third Bank. Fifth Third has multiple channels. Ed Robinson, President of Mortgage Banking for Fifth Third, in a conversation with me, stressed the importance of an "omni-channel experience" that centers on what the consumer wants and needs. He spoke of the need to have an overarching vision from origination through servicing. As a starting point, he believes the focus should be customer engagement and, more importantly, making sure the customer is "able to self-serve, to be in control." High on his list of priorities, too, is maintaining transparency throughout the lifecycle of the process.

As a second step, Ed views Fifth Third's "shop by use" model as a customer-oriented model not unlike visiting a CVS or Walgreens, where customers know how to find the pharmacy and know that their complex concerns can be addressed by the pharmacists. Consistency across the experience, he says, is the key to customer satisfaction. Despite the complexity of multiple channels, Fifth Third found a way to finish second to the best monoline lender in the country.

Never content to rest, Ed is working to re-engineer the lending process to better serve his customers. It's an expensive and painful process, but a necessary step in the life of a maverick.

Learning from Manufacturing

Lenders understand that so much is lost when an experience starts very well, but then gets stuck in the sticky operational works of making a loan. So how does one move away from incremental improvement and achieve a best-in-class, digitally transformed end-to end experience? It's very hard to transform an entire process while still operating the business. Many lenders spoke of innovating within a subset of branches or regions to improve a process, then rolling out to the whole organization. One lender used a unique approach—a "Skunk Works" approach—to test creative ways to improve customer experience and profitability. The maverick CEO related that one needs to free a small group to try new ways and push the envelope regarding technology and process, while remaining compliant. He got that lesson from another industry:

Lockheed's Skunk Works: Conceived in 1943, the Skunk Works division was formed by Kelly Johnson to build America's first jet fighter. German jets had appeared over Europe. Uncle Sam needed a counterpunch, and Johnson got a call. As with virtually all Skunk Works projects that followed, the mission was secretive, and the deadline was remarkably tight. Johnson promised the Pentagon they'd have their first prototype in 150 days. His engineers turned one out in 143 days, creating the P-80 Shooting Star, a sleek, lightning-fast fighter that went on to win history's first jet-versus-jet dogfight over Korea in 1950.

Just four years later, amidst growing fears over a potential Soviet missile attack on the United States, Skunk Works engineers—who often worked ten hours a day, six days a week—created the U-2, the world's first dedicated spy plane. It cruised at 70,000 feet, snapping aerial photographs of Soviet installations. This vital reconnaissance, unobtainable by other means, averted a war in Europe and a nuclear crisis in Cuba.

But high altitude was not enough. By 1960, Soviet radar and surface-to-air missile technology had caught up with the U-2. President Eisenhower needed something quicker, stronger, and more elusive. Using sheets of titanium coated with heat-dissipating black paint, engineers created the SR-71 Blackbird. On July 3, 1963, the plane reached a sustained speed of Mach 3 at astounding 78,000 feet and remains the world's fastest and highest-flying manned aircraft.[33]

[33] http://www.lockheedmartin.com/us/100years/stories/skunk-works.html

The Skunk Works' achievements still continue forward to the present day. The Skunk Works approach, too, may be applicable to mortgage banking. A lender could adopt a "Skunk Works" approach, where successes were rapidly adopted, and failures were contained, as key to making the lender a leader in satisfaction and profitability. A lesson for lenders may be to start with a separate team—including loan officers, processors, underwriters, closers, etc.—whose role is to build a best-in-class process, with multiple disciplines… *and* shield them from non-essential aspects of the team's regular 'day jobs' so they can focus on the best-in-class process and customer service.

Loan Origination Systems

Shopping around for a new loan origination system? You're not alone. According to STRATMOR's 2016 Loan Origination Systems 'LOS' Technology Insight Survey, which polled 266 unique lenders regarding their Loan Origination Systems, 30 percent of respondents are "not satisfied" with their LOS. In fact, 19 percent indicated that they are actively seeking to replace their current LOS and 11 percent reported that they are currently implementing a new LOS. While the report stated 42 percent of respondents were "somewhat satisfied" with their current system, STRATMOR added, "their responses indicate that they are not 'raving fans' of their LOS. Over time we would expect many of these lenders to start to actively look for a new system."

So, where are you? Take out your pen and circle your current feeling about your LOS:

LEVEL OF SATISFACTION			
Completely Satisfied	Somewhat Satisfied	Not Satisfied	Seeking LOS Replacement

If you didn't select "completely satisfied", one should examine why. As a "C" level executive, what are your concerns?

- The LOS is not consumer friendly.

- The LOS is not Loan Officer and/or employee friendly.

- Compliance issues still pop up frequently, costing me time and money.

- The reporting from my LOS doesn't let me manage the business.

- The LOS doesn't help me maximize my profitability.

- My LOS and lending process takes too long from application to investor funding.

- My LOS doesn't help minimize errors, cures, and month end 'fire drills'.

- I'm concerned about the information security aspects of my LOS.

- My LOS provider talks about ROI, but my cost per loan keeps climbing and my profit per loan falls short of my targets.

- Too many checkers checking the checkers.

Changing LOS systems is a big undertaking. Isolate why you've graded your LOS as something other than "Completely Satisfied". How much is driven by factors under your control, and how much by factors out of your control?

Then consider what factors are within your control and what factors are outside of your control. Regulatory changes, GSE changes, and investor overlays are about the only things truly out of your control. Everything else is controllable. Even issues 'out of your control' like regulatory changes are under your influence regarding how you respond, train and adjust your customer experience, process, and workflow.

Now take your pen and go back and circle the shortcomings you've identified on the above list. The shortcomings you've circled above can be the Agenda for a meeting with your key subordinates on how to transform your current business process and workflow, starting with the end in mind. If you take nothing else from this book, prepare your Agenda as above and meet with your team. *Push hard* on the shortcomings—I assure you that you'll *greatly increase your understanding* (for better or worse) of your current process and the impediments your employees and customers deal with every day.

Rob Peterson, Chief Technology Officer of Teraverde®, notes that there are many productivity and process transformation solutions to augment a LOS. "For example, the most popular LOS is Ellie Mae Encompass. This LOS is very configurable. I have seen about 300 instances of Encompass, and the diversity of use and configuration is amazing. The creativity of lenders and their technology partners is impressive. I've seen this LOS support residential real estate lending, commercial lending, chattel lending, construction to permanent lending, fix and flip lending, and a host of other products. The key is knowing the process, and then augmenting the desired process with the correct solutions to support the particular process."

As Rob points out, consider whether your current LOS is customizable or highly configurable. Configurable and customizable do not have the same meaning. A customizable LOS is developed specifically for each lender. The system is static, which means users are stuck with the workflow that was originally implemented. Changing these systems requires either analysts and programmers or contracting with the LOS vendor to modify the system.

A configurable LOS is "out of the box" software and is essentially the same system for all lenders. The LOS can be personalized to the lender's needs. These LOS implementations are usually cloud-based and can be configured by an administrator or by third parties that specialize in configuration. In my view, configurable LOSs is the way of the future for most lenders.

How to tell if your LOS is customizable or configurable? First, the LOS provider will make their case, but the key questions reveal the true nature of your current LOS:

Form-driven or data-driven: Is the LOS form-driven, meaning the screens appear as their equivalent paper forms. (think 1003, 1008, etc.) The LOS requires users to fill forms, increasing the likelihood or errors and increasing the time to complete an application. Many LOSs are form-driven, since usability is easiest for employees as the mortgage forms are familiar. Even form-driven LOS systems can be modified to a data-driven user facing design by creative technologists.

Process and workflow are usually best served if the LOS is configured for data-driven users. That means the flow of work is automated to the greatest extent, and each role in the lender can be configured for how the role inputs information in a normal setting of their work.

Data-driven workflows allow users to populate certain available data automatically; the rest is input in a logical manner in data fields configured for the individual role. The configuration does not force the user to access multiple forms and uses existing and newly input data to automatically populate multiple forms.

Process, Workflow and Task Level control for each role: While a typical loan workflow seems linear from origination, processing, and underwriting to closing, shipping, investor funding, there are tasks that occur that don't fall into this specific sequence. Examples include locking a loan that is floating, repricing a loan where the appraised value is lower than expected, re-disclosing a loan when circumstances change. That's why it's important to have milestones *and* tasks in your workflow, including robotics to perform repetitive tasks, automation to manage tasks and follow-up on completion, and robotic notifications to keep all constituents up to date on the loan progress. Something like a master clock that monitors the timing and process of all tasks, associated milestones, and progress within a loan. Automatically.

Finally, management should have full transparency and the ability to monitor all aspects of the process, workflow and tasks at the loan and role level. Let each employee know what they need to do *right now*. Deal with exceptions before they become a fire drill.

So, if you have a customized LOS, there is a limited amount one can do without technical help from the LOS provider. But if you have a configurable LOS, the doors for substantially improving your process open quickly. In any event, before you give up on your LOS and either opt to replace it or just live with it, consider there is not a "right" LOS. Jerry Schiano, CEO of New Penn Financial, said it best: "I've never met anyone who loved the LOS". But maverick

CEOs can configure their LOS and related systems to be "good enough" to effectively serve their value chain design.

Take the reasons for your dissatisfaction and explore the process, workflow and tasks with your key executives. This is technology, and anything is possible, given time and budget. Be skeptical if you get answers such as "[fill in the name LOS] can't do that". Especially if this feedback comes from your IT people. Al Stanley, CIO of Angel Oak Capital, commented that "A good CIO doesn't stay in his swim lanes. He or she takes an active role in understanding the needs of the business and transforming those needs into action today. A good CIO looks for the 'Yes' answer. The business can't wait for two years for a solution. There needs to be innovation today that serves the business." Al Stanley laughed when I told him one CEO I knew called his CIO a "Chief Interference Officer". Al said he was working hard every day to be regarded as a Chief Innovation Officer.

My favorite response to "can't do that" is to ask, "Even if your job depended on providing this solution?" You'll usually get a more nuanced answer in most cases, describing the constraints, and costs to remediate. If you still get the same "can't do that", you have a Chief Interference Officer on your team.

A CEO asked me why his LOS couldn't provide underwriters the ability to sign off certain documents with an electronic signature. Current practice was print the document, manually sign it, scan it and upload it to the document folder for the loan. The CEO mentioned that his IT team told him, "Can't do this". Actually, you can do it, and the method of doing it isn't difficult. A few days later the underwriters could sign off documents within the LOS and directly place them in the electronic document folder. The CEO mentioned that the improvement saved underwriters about 15 minutes per file, times 400 files per month. For underwriters doing two files a day, the additional 15 minutes per file translates to 12.5 extra underwriting days per month (15 minutes x 400= 100 hours, divided by 8 hours per day = 12.5 underwriting days). That provides 20-25 additional files underwritten at current staffing levels. The CEO said, "It was like adding half an underwriter in productivity" after using the improvement. The lesson is never take, "The LOS (or any system) can't do that". It can. It's just a question of priority and economics.

Sometime a fast and economic approach to transformational business process is to consider whether there are commercially available enhancements that fit. You can add front ends (Blend, BeSmartee, Roostify, SimpleNexus), you can add a scheduling and task management system (Tavant, SpeedPath®), you can add better reporting, (Movation, Coheus™), you can add automation and robotics (Kofax, Coheus™, Tavant). Consider the possibilities to augment your existing LOS, as set out below.

The LOS is not consumer friendly. Depending on your business model and desired customer experience, your LOS may not feel consumer friendly. There are improvements to smooth the front-end process that significantly enhance your borrower experience without junking your LOS, such as Blend, BeSmartee, Roostify, Maxwell, SimpleNexus. Same for TPO front ends.

The LOS is not Loan Officer and/or employee friendly. Some of the front ends have a loan officer role included. Other positions (disclosure, processor, underwriter, closer, shipper, etc.) can have tasks within the workflow automated, streamlined, and simplified. Consider an end-to-end process evaluation to get the most out of your LOS. LOS vendors make continual enhancements, and often times a "re-implementation" can take advantage of inherent capability that is buried in the lender's old processes.

Compliance issues still pop up frequently, costing me time and money. Better end-to-end transformation of the disclosure process and workflow, cure prevention, cure tracking, and integrated prefunding QC can increase profitability and reduce errors.

The reporting from my LOS doesn't let me manage the business. Robust reporting isn't a strong suit for many LOSs. Explore Movation or Coheus™ to add much better visibility and control to your business management. Some, like Coheus™, integrate general ledger, servicing, pricing and hedging systems into a single profit intelligence system.

The LOS doesn't help me maximize my profitability. Most LOS workflows are pre-TRID. Many lender processes and workflows have not been updated for years. A "back-end to front" review of the process and workflow uncovers many issues that can be easily resolved.

My LOS and lending process takes too long from application to investor funding. You get what you measure. As discussed earlier, aggregate numbers don't allow for effective management. You've got to get into employee, branch and loan level metrics to move the profit needle upwards.

My LOS doesn't help minimize errors, cures, and month end 'fire drills'. If your process and workflow don't manage down to the task, loan and employee level, you can't see where the root cause of errors, cures and fire drills occur.

My LOS provider talks about ROI, but my cost per loan keeps climbing and my profit per loan falls short of my targets. Bad process and poor workflow produce bad results. Many of the processes and workflows used by a lender may be pre-TRID. Many may be pre-2007. Some date back before that. In a world where computing cost increases by a factor of two and cost falls by half every 18 months, why does it cost twice as much to do a loan in 2017 as in 2010? Too much human spackle!

Too many checkers checking the checkers. Checkers checking checkers is bad process, bad workflow, and bad business. Imagine how many people would be in the cockpit of an airline if the airline didn't use automation, robotics, and task level controls through all phases (i.e., milestones) of a flight. The two pilots on the flight deck of each commercial airline collectively fly over 10,000 flights a day, every day, in all weather, and rarely have an accident. Incidents are managed and many never come to the attention of the passengers. But there are no checkers checking checkers in the cockpit. Good process, workflow, task management, good instruments and reporting systems and consistent training enable this enviable safety record.

Get the checkers checking checkers out of your organization, and replace them with good process, workflow, task control, service levels, and real-time reporting and management. If you have a vision, intended culture, and desired customer experience in mind, it's easier to accomplish than most think. Start at the end of the process, describing the destination in terms of customer experience, service levels, desired profitability and desired quality levels. Then work forward, defining process, workflow, and task as you get to the very first touchpoint – the Customer's Initial Interest in getting a loan from you.

CHAPTER FOUR
Technological Transformation

As we proceed from workflow to technology, we need to agree on one point as an industry—FinTech is an essential element of the future of mortgage banking. In summary, we can define "FinTech" as the technology platforms servicing the Financial Services Industry. As we discussed earlier, an ever-increasing number of consumers are expecting more advanced interactions and a more streamlined, technological process in their consumer experiences. More to the point (and more salient to our search for a streamlined industry), however, FinTech is essential for mortgage banking as an efficiency tool, and one that can help ameliorate the enormous cost and complexities of the loan manufacturing process.

Some technology is emergent and holds great promise in terms of lowering costs and providing a trusted source of data without the need for re-verification. Much clarity can come from understanding the emerging technologies that will likely change the landscape of mortgage banking. It would also behoove us to understand when and where these technology transformations are likely to disrupt the industry, and how to make these tools work for us, as individuals and as an industry.

It's also essential to look at the cultural disruption FinTech will introduce to mortgage banking. What will these technologies change in terms of customer relationships and loan officers? Will they really have a favorable profit impact? Will robots replace processors?

Let's start with something that's still some years away from widespread adoption. Blockchain technology is the future, albeit not the immediate future. Like most things defined as the "future", it is still cost prohibitive for many, unfortunately, and adoption by the average user will take time. It does, however, promise to be an elegant solution to data integrity and introduces the possibility of eliminating "checkers checking the checkers". It has to be a part of the conversation moving forward in the mortgage banking space.

The Future and Blockchain

Henry Santos was responsible for the mortgage financial services vertical at IBM. Henry kindly invited me to a session at IBM's Thomas J. Watson Research Center to delve into blockchain with a small group of financial executives. The discussion below is publicly available information from that session and follow-on discussions.

What does blockchain do? According to IBM, blockchain is a shared unchangeable ledger for recording the history of transactions. In mortgage banking, these transactions could include the receipt of trusted borrower information, such as bank account data, income data, and related qualifying information. The data comes from a trusted source (such as a bank, the IRS, or payroll service) and never needs to be re-verified.

Blockchain is *Distributed*. It works as a system of record that is shared among participants of the business network, eliminating the need to reconcile disparate ledgers. It is *Permissioned*, such that each member of the network has access rights so that confidential information is shared on a need-to-know basis. It is *Secured*. Consensus is required from all network members and all validated transactions are permanently recorded. No one, not even a system administrator, can delete or change information[34].

For example, the bank account records (say 24 months of transaction data) can be provided by a bank to a mortgage blockchain regarding a borrower. Same for payroll data. (*Data*, not images.) Same for credit report data. One now has *trusted source* data regarding a borrower that is immutable and can be utilized by authorized parties. Same for mortgage payment history, prior credit events, collateral information, etc. This authenticated history is permissioned, meaning a consumer could grant permission to a lender to access this trusted information.

The consumer's record could also be *appended in real time*. Meaning once the basis information is created, the ongoing transactional history could be built. Imagine having an authenticated complete history of a consumer's finances available for an instant credit decision since all of the information is assembled form trusted parties! No redundant QC. No robotics. Just authentic real-time data.

---

[34] https://www.ibm.com/blockchain/what-is-blockchain.html

Access to this information could be granted by the customer to servicers, prospective originators, owners of the underlying loan, etc. This means the party owning the servicing could essentially offer a refinance or additional credit or wealth management services if the consumer grants permission. The servicing asset takes on a whole new dimension as an element of the financial value chain in mortgage lending. It's not just a stream of cash flows... it's access to everything financial about the customer.

Will the GSEs emerge as the host of mortgage blockchain services? The power and scope of blockchain is also why Dave Stevens of the MBA feels so strongly about the "Bright Line" between primary originations and secondary market agencies. The GSEs will likely be one of the sponsors of authenticated data, and the step from *buying* loans to *making* loans could be a very small step indeed. Blockchain's promise is speed, reduced cost and the promise of truly seamless fast decisions on new credit in the mortgage lending process.

Henry Santos envisioned a blockchain-powered utility that essentially collates and distributes trusted source digital information without copying it. This solves the almost mind-numbing problem of how to protect sensitive financial data. After the Equifax breach, this issue is a clear and present danger to any industry and to the consumer. It can also serve as a highly efficient tracker, allowing individuals and companies to view the entire history of a financial transaction.

Such technologies enable the servicing asset to be monetized in many ways. The entire history of the customer's mortgage(s) and related information could be easily utilized. Imagine having a complete digital record of the customer's application data, with all servicing and payment transaction available to the servicer. What if the customer "opted in" to let the servicer obtain a digital stream of bank transactions and payroll data. One could then literally do a refinance at the touch of a mouse. Or obtain a new mortgage needing only an appraisal. Or maybe no appraisal is even needed at all.

Depending on the location of the new home, the GSEs may waive an appraisal. Add in social media, and life's events can be coupled to the factual financial record. My attorney son and his wife are expecting a new daughter, and they are looking for a new property in the Bay Area. If I were his lender and discovered those facts, could I jump on the needs for financing for a new home? It may sound farfetched, but, if one looks for a product on Google, Amazon, or other provider, see how many times a provider of that product pops up in ads as one continues around social media or the Web.

That may be out in the future, but the power of blockchain and related technologies should inform our business process of today. Some precursors to a full blockchain implementation are already at hand: Fannie Mae Day 1 Certainty.

Day 1 Certainty

Andrew Bon Salle, Executive Vice President for Single Family at Fannie Mae describes how the alphabet soup such as UMDP, UAD, UCDP, URLA, UCD led to Day 1 Certainty:

> *[These acronyms] represent industry-wide efforts to create uni-form data standards, and the work to adopt them has been a pain point for lenders. But these efforts also reflect a long-overdue investment in data quality and efficiency. Now, we are beginning to see the return on investment. Thanks to data standardization and uniformity, lenders can now get Day*

1 Certainty™ – freedom from representations and warranties on key loan components plus more speed and simplicity.

Less than a decade ago, residential appraisal reports were not even digitized, with no standard formats even for simple things like dates. Property condition was described in wildly nonstandard, free-form terms such as "Average New," "Average Old," and "Typical." The number of bathrooms in a property might be listed as 1.5 or 1.1, both meaning a full and a half bath.

The Uniform Appraisal Dataset (UAD) standardized appraisal data, and since 2012 Fannie Mae has required digitized appraisal reports. With that foundation, we developed Collateral Underwriter® (CU™). Lenders receive freedom from representations and warranties on the appraised property value on eligible loans with a CU risk score of 2.5 or lower – about 60 percent of all appraisals submitted to Fannie Mae. Enhanced Property Inspection Waivers (PIWs) provide offers to waive an appraisal on about 20 percent of limited cash-out refinances. Lenders get freedom from representations and warranties on property value, condition, and marketability.

Combine standardization with so-called 'big data' and that's the power behind the Desktop Underwriter® (DU®) validation service – another Day 1 Certainty offering. Data power enables a simpler, more accurate digital process. With electronic validation of income, assets, and employment, lenders and borrowers benefit by moving away from the manual processes prevalent in the industry today."[35]

[35] http://www.fanniemae.com/portal/research-insights/perspectives/day-1-certainty-bon-salle-030217.html

According to HousingWire[36], on October 23, 2017, Fannie Mae introduced its new Single Source Validation, a service that is now on pilot, which allows lenders to validate a borrower's income, assets and employment through one report using source data rather than multiple paper documents. The company explained this step will amplify savings and make it easier to originate loans. Its new Application Programming Interface platform will allow lenders to utilize Fannie Mae's data and technology solutions to quickly access the full set of Desktop Underwriter Messages data, driving greater efficiency. Finally, its new Servicing Marketplace will connect servicers to sellers who are interested in partnering with each other for serving transfers when sellers sell loans to Fannie Mae, giving more transparency in the system while removing cost and friction.

Day 1 Certainty and Single Source will likely be a big part of the future. The difficulty and challenges facing both customers and lenders is that the success rate for seeking income information through Day 1 Certainty, according to my informal discussions with lenders, is 15% or less. Sometimes, much less. Lenders also relate that a significant portion of customers are unwilling to provide their log on credentials for bank and investment accounts, largely due to security concerns. The Equifax breach has added to this concern. Day 1 Certainty and Single Source (and similar efforts) are very large steps forward and they will ultimately improve transparency and speed in mortgage lending. But high success rates for willing borrowers is in the future. Confidence to provide credentials varies considerably. These hurdles, however, will be overcome as consumer comfort with providing credentials increases, more payroll providers optimize the matching process, and banks standardize the period of assets reported (currently ranging from 2 months to 2 years).

[36] https://www.housingwire.com/articles/41638-fannie-mae-reveals-major-upgrade-to-its-day-1-certainty-product

Maybe blockchain *isn't* that far off... and Dave Stevens' definition of the Bright Line between GSEs and primary originators is a very real need for the mortgage banking industry.

So better, trusted data is on its way. In the meantime, how does one get more out of older technology—the LOS—today?

It's important to deploy technology after working through all of the elements, including process and workflow. Jonathan Corr notes that the Encompass LOS (as do many other competing products) has great flexibility:

> *Encompass is an off the shelf [configurable] solution that you can get deployed very quickly. A lender configures it. Extends it in a very robust way. And still be able to upgrade it, which is very unique from other systems. But you can also get yourself into trouble if you don't think [process and workflow] through and document well.*[37]*" My discussion with Jonathan focused on thinking through the customer and employee experience, designing process and workflow, and then implementing technology.*
>
> *That's what some of the best lenders that I've seen in terms of implementations do, and they've had thousands of dollars in savings per loan. And then you put yourself in a great position to move forward and evolve because you've thought about your process. As you change a process, be very disciplined about how you think about it upfront. You*

---

[37] There are many good LOS systems available. Jonathan Corr was very gracious in providing extended access to both his views, industry data and members of his executive team. Mr. Corr's views on Encompass can easily be extended to other LOS systems offered by competitors.

want to think outside the box. Don't take an application and wrap it around your old processes. One of the reasons you embrace new technology is to do things differently, to provide a better experience for your consumers more efficiently. So, take that opportunity and document it.

Jonathan also added that lenders that simply take their existing processes and add technology are often disappointed. This is consistent with my own experience. Changing LOS without thoughtfully contemplating the current and future vision, customer experience, workflow, and desired performance metrics of the lender's business plan leads to disappointment.

We spoke about the cost of manufacturing a loan versus manufacturing a car. Jonathan continued:

One of the things that you just mentioned earlier about GM it just like any of the manufacturing process. If you are building in quality from the beginning, you're going to have that much less rework as you get further into the process. You're going to lower your costs.

From a Fannie Mae standpoint, it also increases the likelihood you're going to deliver it to them [a loan file] they like." A fully documented process using technology to leverage process and workflow reduces costs, speeds approval, and reduces repurchase risk.

Should a CEO undertake a complete redesign *and implementation* of the entire process at once, including fully aiming for a complete 'Digital Mortgage' solution? The answer is a resounding, "no". It's critical to understand what parts of the customer experience, process, and workflow will be modified first. Many of the CEOs I spoke with cautioned about trying to do too much at once. Have a roadmap of customer experience, process, and workflow that you wish to automate more fully. Work sequentially to add the most value for a given process first, and then work through to completion.

Nima Ghamsari, CEO of Blend, stated:

I think the biggest, the hardest part…. there's always this nirvana view of the future, of 'here's how good this could be if we solved all these problems at once'. That has two sorts of pitfalls to it that I think are worth thinking about for companies that are undergoing this journey. The first is not every problem has been solved by companies that are out there. There's a long way to go. There's a lot more to solve. And the industry is enormous. There are so many participants. There are so many parts of the process." Meaning, that having a clear roadmap of the customer experience, process, and workflow lets one deploy solutions to the most pressing issues now and then undergo continuous improvement to reach the ultimate destination. So many projects fail by attempting to implement segments that are just too large.

If we waited for everybody to solve all these things before we released our product, we'd be having this conversation in 2030. It would be a long time before we solved it. But also, what that means for the organization is that even within the organization they don't even need to use everything that we or others have to get started. So, by that I mean [some lenders] need everything integrated and everything perfect before I get started. But actually, the incremental value and the incremental benefit to your customers, if you're a financial institution, of getting something up and running that allows [customers] to get that simplicity and transparency is big enough on its own.

Said another way, it's important to have the overall experience, process, and workflow documented, but undertake implementation in steps.

I think a big key success metric in my mind is how do you [implement] in a way that doesn't take two, three, four years, which is historically how long it's taken to do software changes. I think it's important from the perspective of these financial institutions that iterating is the new way of building software. Small chunks, small bites. Constant improvement towards the right vision, towards that perfect Nirvana world that everyone wants... but don't wait for the Nirvana world before you make a move.

Nima's observations make it critically important that the overall experience, process, and workflow be understood and documented so that the highest value technology components can be implemented first.

Tim Nguyen, CEO of BeSmartee had some interesting observations on the challenges of cost to produce and lender profitability:

I think you break it down to three different buckets. Compliance is definitely a big factor. We have to comply with the law. And the law is complicated. You know many different rules [regarding] timing issues that we have to deal with. So, compliance is definitely one thing.

Number two is the competitive landscape where Loan Officer compensation is really a big cost. When you look at the Stratmor Group numbers, I think 60 or 70 percent of the cost goes out to the originator. It's tough to differentiate yourselves, to compete.

[Number three], lenders' incentive to drive that cost down hasn't truly been there.

In other words, the industry as a whole has seen costs rise from $5,000 per loan to $8,800 per loan, and everyone is affected. Lenders become numb to the aggregate cost because everyone had to shoulder the same costs.

But what happened if a lender began to push on the cost buckets? Could the cost be reduced to $5,000 per loan, or less?

The State of Fintech

The state of FinTech has to begin with a discussion on data integrity. "Dirty data" or missing data is responsible for much of the rework and underlying defects in mortgage banking. Maylin Casanueva, Chief Operating Officer at Teraverde® observed, "Data integrity in mortgage banking is a far cry from what it should be. The amount of missing or erroneous data throughout the process can cause major reductions in profitability. As we review data in lender systems, the basics seem to be there, but a close review still reveals data integrity issues in computation of income, in computation of liquid reserves and missing ancillary data. Coheus™ (a profit intelligence solution primarily designed by Ms. Casanueva) rapidly identifies 'dirty' and missing data. I'm surprised how dirty data can be. The root cause of much missing and 'dirty' data is the manual efforts in mortgage banking. These manual efforts need to be replaced with a data-driven approach to quality. Second to data integrity is the poor quality of operational and financial performance data. Many lenders don't key in on the key drivers of profitability and attainment of service levels."

Ms. Casanueva observed that much can be done to improve document management. "The ability to visually classify documents and extract key data elements from these documents exists today. This technology can greatly increase the efficiency of the mortgage lending process, especially in Third Party Origination and Whole Loan Sale/Purchase transactions. One can ingest an unindexed PDF file of 800 pages, visually classify the file, index it, extract key data from the digital images, and identify errors or potential data integrity issues without any human "stare and compare" review. Best of all, the visually classified documents can be integrated into an LOS, and also permanently stored for enterprise access throughout the life of the loan. This capability exists today."

With that said, what is the state of deployed technology in mortgage banking today? And what are the innovations that are beginning to transform the industry? Stratmor[38] recently conducted a survey regarding lender adoption of digital mortgage strategies. The top five strategies that lenders have in production or in development are:

- the ability for the borrower to execute disclosures online;

- online borrower satisfaction surveys;

---

[38] Stratmor is a well-established consulting firm serving the mortgage lending industry.

- the ability for the borrower to upload documents and respond to conditions;

- online lead management or CRM systems that enable originators to nurture relationships over an extended timeline; and,

- the ability to submit appraisal data for agency review for representation and warranty relief.

While promising in some sense, this is a far cry from the totally integrated approach that Amazon takes with the sales and fulfillment process and its customers. Clearly, the industry has a long way to go. For those resistant to adopting new technologies, the argument is pretty persuasive with regards to the bottom line, too. There is considerable evidence in the gain on sale ("GOS") margins for lenders that suggests that price is not the main element for competing for customers in most cases. Rather there is evidence that competition is shifting towards providing borrowers a satisfying complete and superior customer experience—something that interested parties cannot achieve without technology.

The Leaders in the Space

While progress has been slow, there are many startups and established leaders in the space who are pushing the boundaries when it comes to FinTech in mortgage banking.

Any conversation around FinTech in mortgage banking naturally turns to Quicken. Quicken has not only leveraged technology in a transformative way in our space, but also has made sure that the consumer is aware that tech is digitally transforming access to mortgages. Since Quicken's launch of Rocket Mortgage and its Super Bowl launch advertisements, borrowers can clearly see that online options for the completion of a mortgage are available. Quicken's advertising has become so ubiquitous that it's not only on television, but also Facebook, Google search, and a variety of other websites. Rocket Mortgage is even advertised at gas station gas pumps through GSTV (GSTV stand for 'gas station television', a display screen and audio activated while pumping gas. GSTV is another venture of Dan Gilbert, owner of Quicken Loans).

Borrowers have virtually unlimited ability to research lenders online either through direct inquiry, or through a variety of lead sources, or through aggregation sites such as Zillow and Realtor.com. The borrowers are ready, so when will the mortgage industry respond and follow in the path of companies such as Quicken?

FinTech as Facilitator

FinTech companies have an established history at this point as facilitators to financial service providers. Some FinTech companies such as Social Finance or Lending Club are integrated technology and lending platforms aimed at non-mortgage consumer lending, for example. Lending Club also offers transparency as to loan metrics and performance. One can access anonymized credit metrics of every loan made by Lending Club, the loan pricing, and credit performance. This data can be used by loan investors to evaluate the risk/reward of Lending Club's loan platform. Since the mortgage banking process is much more complex and highly regulated than consumer lenders, uncovering and understanding where FinTech fits in is more problematic. There are those out there, however, who are finding a viable place and making transformative noise in the space.

While the list is getting longer, three companies in particular have been making significant progress. BeSmartee, Blend, and Roostify are bringing an Amazon-like *front end* experience to borrowers, from Initial Interest to Application funneling them efficiently from their initial interest in a loan through the application process. They have been some of the first to understand how technology can improve customer experience and, as an extension, increase ROI.

This is an important point that we in the mortgage industry need to keep in mind when it comes to FinTech—few innovators, if any, are suggesting backing off from the tradition of the high touch of the loan officer. Many envision technology as empowering the LO. As Tim Nguyen put it, "People will always talk to a loan officer. It is our job to make that easier. It makes the loan officer more efficient."

Big Data and Artificial Intelligence are also doing their part to transform the mortgage application process and are utilized to auto-populate fields. Borrowers "can utilize multiple options to communicate via any computer or mobile device and support through built-in chat, email, and screen-sharing features."

Blend makes a direct pitch of a digital experience to the borrower: "The home buying process is digital, like the rest of your financial life." Borrowers need an application experience they've come to expect: *faster, smarter, easier.* Blend (and others) promote a familiar home buyer experience, again invoking the Amazon-like shopping experience. Borrowers can provide needed documentation to lenders through quick, secure connectivity with trusted financial institutions, payroll, and tax providers.

The common denominators of these front-end products are web and mobile application capability, contextual paths through the process, integration with financial service and data providers to access borrower financial, employment and credit data, and automated approvals. Consumer disclosure and continued contact are options that can be selected by the lender.

Compared to the Stratmor digital capabilities of lenders in its survey, these third party FinTech companies provide a quantum leap over the core digital mortgage features noted in the Stratmor survey. Clearly, the race is on for a more Amazon-like customer experience. But the front end experience can be compromised if the overall fulfillment capabilities of a lender are not designed to integrate and support the front end.

But again, it all comes back to consumer satisfaction. Tim Nguyen put it best during our discussion around this book. "Technology is not the end all. It's simply a platform... the process, the people, the core values come into play... technology has to be done in a way that supports the consumer but doesn't leave them out to be by all by themselves."

The fact that technological innovation is required and long past due in the mortgage industry is clear to many. As Bill Emerson put it, "All one has to do is take a look at the millennial generation and the way that they consume information and the way that they interact to realize that if we don't embrace technology as an industry we are going to get left behind ... it would be a shame to see experienced mortgage lenders lose market share because they were too slow to adopt what's right in front of their face." This need to serve an increasing technologically-capable borrower base is also recognized by Ed Robinson, Nathan Burch, Rich Bennion, and many other maverick CEOs.

What are the consumers of this new, tech-savvy generation looking for? As discussed earlier, fast answers and control.

One way in which the technological innovators in the mortgage industry are addressing this is by developing ways to have the consumer manage his or her data as opposed to just *provide* his or her data. While this is transformative in many ways in that it unifies the front-end process, getting accurate data with integrity proves difficult. As Tim Nguyen put it, "The more you empower consumers, the more accurate data has to be, because you can't sit there and filter everything and do everything for the consumer anymore. The more power the consumer has, the smarter those tools have to be. It's about managing the data not providing the data. We want to turn you [the customer] into a data verifier not a data provider."

It costs $8,800 to create a new mortgage loan, with just $190 spent on technology. That's just six basis points of cost, and far behind the approximately 200 basis points in compensation per loan, according to MBA data. Individuals and companies across the industry are hesitant to move forward with technology and expand investment. What is holding us back? Is it a lack of understanding of what is out there? Is it demonstrated disappointment with LOS technology? The STRATMOR survey run in 2016 showed that only 42 percent of respondents were *somewhat satisfied* with their LOS.[39] Why has the promise of FinTech in mortgages been languishing and what is the real and measurable ROI we can expect from it?

[39] http://www.stratmorgroup.com/wp-content/uploads/STRATMOR-Insights-December-2016.pdf

FinTech & the Loan Officer

An interesting piece in TechCrunch highlighted some of the difficulties facing FinTech as it tries to transform mortgages.[40] One particularly salient point addresses the fact that FinTech solutions must integrate with legacy systems; as such, much FinTech in the mortgage industry addresses niche concerns, rather than taking an overarching, transformative approach.

There is also the issue of volume, also referenced by TechCrunch. One jarring statistic is that the top loan officer[41] in the country as of 2015 originated nearly $645 million in loans, outpacing even high-performing tech startups in the space.

This issue—the fact that LOs still dominate when it comes to volume—may account for some of the cultural resistance from some in the mortgage industry to FinTech. It's true that some people just won't change. There is a very successful loan officer that I know who still takes an application with a pen. She refuses to use technology, saying, "It gets between me and the customer". The lender who employs her is willing to accept her as employable because she takes a complete application, structures loans effectively, and fosters solid relationships with customers. The same cannot be said for the staff that works with her, since they take the brunt of translating

[40] https://techcrunch.com/2016/04/21/why-startups-cant-disrupt-the-mortgage-industry/

[41] The "Top Loan Officer(s)" are generally teams of junior originators, operations staff all reporting to the "Top Loan Officer". My experience with this type of top loan officer is they thinks they own their teams and customers, and often act as if they owned my company. One seasoned and cynical executive defined mortgage banking as "the systematic transfer of loan revenue and shareholder capital from shareholders to loan officers, who bear no risk with respect to repurchase, prepayment or regulatory actions."

the hand-written app to a closed loan. There are other loan officers just like her who remain employed because they connect with the customer, structure a loan correctly, and take a complete application with documents "the old-fashioned way". The CEO of the lender who employs her says, "She takes a good application, has good volume, structures well, does a lot of govvie and is profitable, even with the additional staff that has to walk her loans through our LOS."

It seems to me—and to many of the thought leaders with whom I spoke—that there is also a fear that FinTech will eliminate human touch, ultimately endangering the customer service that is essential to the process. But evidence is that adoption of technology does not interfere with customer relationships, but instead can enhance it.

In the online world, the standard of excellence may be the Amazon experience. The Amazon experience is tightly integrated, from the customer's first point of contact right through to ease of shipping. Take a look at the business model of Amazon[42]. Think back to the lending process model from a few pages back. Which model is clearer?

---

[42] Adopted from Alexander Osterwalden, Business Model Canvas, SlideShare.Net

AMAZON'S BUSINESS MODEL CANVAS				
KEY PARTNERS	**KEY ACTIVITIES**	**VALUE PROPOSITION**	**CUSTOMER RELATIONSHIP**	**CUSTOMER SEGMENT**
Logistics Partner	Merchandising	Convenience	Self-Service	Individual Leverage
Affiliates	Production and Design	Price	Automated Services	Group Leverage
Authors and Publishers	**KEY RESOURCES**	Instant Fulfillment with eReader	**DISTRIBUTION CHANNELS**	Global Consumer Market
Network of Sellers	Physical Warehouses	Vast Selection	Affiliates	
	Human, Web Application & Development		Application Interfaces	
			Amazon.com	
			Sale of Assets	

COST STRUCTURE	**REVENUE STREAMS**
Low Cost Structure	E-books and Content
IT and Fulfillment Infrastructure	Acquisitions and Investments
Economies of Scale	Commission on Reseller Sales

Amazon offers a 'one-click' buying experience through which a customer finds what they want and—with a click—get that item on its way to their front door. The real differentiator in this experience is that Amazon keeps the customer informed at every point along the way, keeping the customer up to speed on when the product will ship and following up with status updates to and through receipt of the product by the consumer. Whether the product is flawless or flawed, the consumer also has the ability to review the product, the seller, and the customer experience in an instant. The customer, too, has an easy way to return products that don't fit his or her needs. All of this comes in one place, and in a familiar user interface.

With Amazon setting the customer experience expectation, lenders have a tall order of business when it comes to defining the digital mortgage retail experience in addition to the traditional retail experience and the direct to consumer experience. How far does the experience extend into the process, and how will a lender provide a simple, fast, and easy buying experience? Lenders also need to consider factors such as product selection, speed to approval, and time to closing in the mix. If the experience is face to face, how will all interactions after the initial face-to-face take place? How will follow-up, loan status, additional information, appraisal results, and third-party management take place? How will the realtor or builder stay updated on progress along the way?

Are most of Amazon's customers Millennials? Baby Boomers? The Tech Chart of the Day[43] below suggested broad adoption of technology solutions when they are easy to use and provide obvious value. Customers over age 60 are the second highest user group (by age) of Amazon Prime as of 2014, meaning they are invested in using the broad reach of Amazon Prime (free shipping, some free video on demand, streaming music on demand).

---

[43] http://www.businessinsider.com/amazon-prime-demographics-chart-2015-1

AGE DISTRIBUTION OF AMAZON'S US CUSTOMERS
(US, 2014)

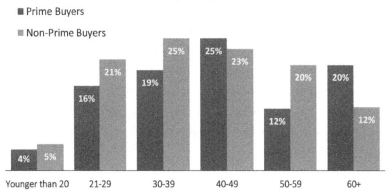

■ Prime Buyers

▨ Non-Prime Buyers

Source: comScore and Business Insider

Year to date 2017 data suggests that 26% of Amazon Prime customer are over 55 years old[44], with 39% of Prime customers being Millennials, Gen X and Gen Y (18-34), and the remaining 35% of Prime customers between 35 and 54. To me, this means a significant portion of the U.S. population, regardless of age, have adopted Amazon as a primary source of researching and purchasing their needs. They've committed $99 to buy Prime for a year. My Texas Hold'em playing son tells me they are "pot committed"[45], meaning they've invested financially and emotionally in the service *and* they are going to use it.

---

[44] https://www.statista.com/statistics/304940/amazon-prime-us-age-distribution/

[45] Generally speaking, being pot committed means having arrived at a point in a poker hand at which folding to any bet or raise has become an incorrect play. Such a situation is determined by pot odds and how those odds compare to your chances of winning a hand. (https://www.pokernews.com/strategy/understanding-what-it-means-to-be-pot-committed-20050.htm)

In 2012, just after Prime was launched, Prime customers were about four percent (about 7.5 million) of Amazon's 182 million active customer base. But they accounted for nearly 10 percent of purchases, because they spend more than twice as much as non-prime customers—$1,224 a year versus $505.[46] In 2017, according to Business Insider, *85 million customers* had signed up for Prime. And Prime customers tend to spend just under twice that of non-prime customers. $1,300 per year for Prime, versus $700 for non-prime. Amazon recognized a "pot committed" strategy, and it is rewarding Amazon well.

If Amazon can create that kind of growth and commitment, what is achievable as a lender? How can a lender get a customer to be "pot committed", as they say? There's a lesson from commercial banking—core deposits. According to Investopedia, "Core deposits are the deposits made in a bank's natural demographic market. Banks count on core deposits as a stable source of funds for their lending base. Core deposits offer many advantages to banks, such as predictable costs and a measurement of the degree of customer loyalty." Core deposits are generally checking accounts and money market accounts. These accounts are transactional and provide low or no-cost deposits to fund the bank's assets.

Many bankers believe core deposits are "sticky" because of great product design, good marketing, etc. "As retail banks continue to brace for the digital future, branches are still having a significant effect on customer satisfaction across all customer age groups", according to the J.D. Power 2017 U.S. Retail Banking Satisfaction Study[47]. (SM)

---

[46] http://www.businessinsider.com/amazon-prime-10-million-members-morningstar-2013-3

[47] http://www.jdpower.com/press-releases/jd-power-2017-us-retail-banking-satisfaction-study

The study finds that overall retail bank satisfaction is significantly higher among customers who have visited a branch within the past 12 months vs. those who have only used digital channels. Within the closely watched Millennial age group (those born from 1982-1994), satisfaction is highest when bank customers use both branch and digital banking channels. This is consistent with the J.D. Power research on when both digital and personal interactions, of the customers' choice, occur in mortgage lending.

My own opinion after just having changed banks (due to a poorly executed bank merger by my former bank) is that changing a checking account is very difficult and painful. Direct payroll deposit, ACH, bill pay accounts, etc. all must be changed, among other things. Core deposits are core because it costs a customer time and energy to change banks. A checking account has become a low-tech digital wallet. One gets used to it, it works well enough, and inexorably one gets "pot committed" to the bank and its checking account. It's not bank marketing or product brilliance.

There are other examples of "pot committed" products, such as Google (Gmail, GoogleDocs, Chrome), etc. So again, how does a lender entice a customer to foment this type of relationship with a product? How can the relationship get so deep that the customer will naturally seek the lender out? Or how will the lender anticipate the customer needs to the product or service so that it arrives just as the customer detects the need? As Steve Jobs once said of the iPhone, paraphrased, the iPhone solves customer needs that the customer didn't even know they had.

Stan Middleman thinks the servicing relationship is the key to getting a customer "pot committed". He observes:

Not too many years ago our industry was dominated by the largest banks. Ninety percent of the servicing was in possession of the five largest banks. Today, that has certainly spread around and been diffused, and non-banks are as prevalent in the top 10 mortgage banks as banks are. Some of the changes that we see tend to put business in the hands of more entrepreneurial folks rather than institutional people and banks. I think that that will help them innovate, tactically, the approach to the consumer. ...Someday in the not horribly distant future, getting a loan will be much faster. The ability to get a loan much faster and much easier will lend consumers to be much more subject to the law of inertia and have a propensity to stay with the lender that they're with.

Stan anticipates innovations that streamline the process, slash wait times and processing times as key drivers for consumers. "If you could go to your computer, type in three lines, and all that information that you're required to have is already readily available to your lender and it takes two minutes, five minutes... I think you're going to tend to want to stay there." In other words, the inertia of core deposits holds true for a complete dataset available to a lender to make a new mortgage transaction very easy for a customer to complete.

Who gets there first is anyone's guess at this point. Stan continues. "I'm not sure it'll be the banks, or it will be the non-banks, but I think somebody will emerge with the clients, and I believe that we're kind of in an arms race."

Ultimately, though no one is suggesting backing off from the tradition of the high touch of the loan officer. Many envision technology as empowering the LO. Tim Nguyen says, "People will always talk to a loan officer. It is our job to make that just easier. It makes the loan officer more efficient."

Stan Middleman of Freedom Mortgage had an interesting perspective on FinTech in the mortgage industry. Rather than driving innovation, Stan feels the industry will need to function essentially as an early adopter of FinTech, such as Day 1 Certainty and Single Source driven by GSEs. Any innovation, he believes, has to start there.

Mr. Middleman continues:

> I think it's important to recognize one fundamental fact—in the United States, the government fundamentally finances 95 percent of all homeownership... Fannie and Freddie are actually starting to compete in terms of technology. As that starts to change, I think we'll be forced to be most effective as early adopters, rather than innovators.
>
> As long as the government is going to subsidize housing finance, the driver of the technological improvements will be the agencies. And the companies that are gathering up the servicing for those agencies are going to be, I think, the beneficiaries of that activity.

This view is similar to my own; that is, the GSEs will provide the information utility, whether blockchain or not, and the value of servicing will become more dependent on the relationship value as opposed to the mortgage cash flows. And it's already well underway at Fannie Mae with Day 1 Certainty and Single Source, and at other FinTech products that provide direct access to a trusted data source that does not have to be reverified.

CHAPTER FIVE

The Maverick's Approach to Financial Performance

W hen I ask a mortgage banker about their business, the first quantitative description that is mentioned is dollar volume of originations. A natural answer, since that scopes out the basic scale of the operation. But volume is not a description of the lender's profitability, health, cash flow, or long-term viability.

It's not an industry secret—many mortgage bankers are enthralled by volume. Entry into the top 100 or top 10 lenders is an aspirational goal for many, and it has set the standard of success for decades. Is this devotion to volume over profit beneficial to the mortgage banking industry in the long run?

Some lenders view volume as a metric of success. One CEO (not in the Maverick interview group) that I spoke with considered the billion dollar threshold to be a "rite of passage". Another had crossed the $1 billion mark and was now aiming at the $10 billion mark.

When I ask a CEO about profit, the answer is usually, "we're better than peer". Statistically, half the time this may be true. The other half of the time, it is not. Not everyone can be "better than peer". C level executives of lenders don't seem to focus on profit as much as other industries, according to Martin Kerr of Loan Vision. The exception is publicly traded lenders, where profitability is transparent due to public reporting requirements. Why is profit so much more important than volume?

"Speed is Life" —that's the saying of fighter pilots. Speed is energy, and it can be converted to altitude quickly, or used in evasive maneuvering. Every fighter pilot knows that speed is life. Similarly, "profit is life" for all lenders, public or private. *Profit is the sole long-term source of capital and positive cash flow for most non-publicly traded lenders.* Without profit, cash flow will be lacking.

Most lenders realize profit and cash flow are not equivalent. For example, Mortgage Servicing Rights ("MSRs") generate income when originated, but the cash flow is initially negative. Investment in "MSRs" is a use of cash. The investment yields a periodic flow of servicing fees, and some cash arising from escrow balances. Non-performing servicing can rapidly become a heavy use of cash, as investors require timely principal and interest payments, and taxes and insurance must be paid whether the borrower is current or delinquent. These requirements can adversely affect the cash flow and underlying liquidity[48] of a lender.

---

[48] Cash flow is a measurement of the sources and uses of cash. Profit is the measurement of income (both cash and accruals of income) and expenses (both cash and accruals of expense). Liquidity is the availability of cash to pay expenses and obligations. A company can be profitable on a generally accepted accounting principle basis but have little or no cash. An example is a company that has heavily invested in MSRs, using its available cash. The result is lack of liquidity (meaning lack of liquid assets such as cash. MSRs are not considered a source of short term liquidity, as they cannot be converted to immediate cash).

Generally accepted accounting principles ("GAAP") for mortgage banking can produce timing differences in profit versus cash flow. MSRs discussed previously are an example where income is recognized at creation of the MSR, but the cash flow arising from servicing fees occurs over the life of the loan.

The recognition of fair value of locked loans may produce profit, but it does not generate immediate cash flow. Lenders that hedge secondary market transactions (as opposed to best efforts forward sales) can realize fair value profit from mark to market of the hedging derivatives. Publicly traded lenders contend with the SEC's Staff Accounting Bulletin 109 "Written Loan Commitments Recorded at Fair Value through Earnings". This application of GAAP may generate timing differences between profit recognition and cash flow. Generally, these timing differences span less than 90 days, as they relate the origination and funding cycle of the underlying loans. We'll cover profit versus cash flow timing differences—short term differences arising from the origination and funding cycle, and long-term differences related to servicing—a little later in this chapter.[49]

The basic equation, however, is that profit is the sole long-term source of capital growth and positive cash flow. Company, channel, region, and branch profitability are extremely important in managing a lender's business. A little secret—if an executive is a little defensive or self-conscious reading the last few paragraphs

---

[49] There are also profit versus cash flow differences arising to taxable income, deferred taxes, depreciation and amortization of long term assets, mortgage servicing rights, loan loss reserve as well as taxation differences arising from the form of business organization, such as a "C" corporation, "S" corporation, limited liability companies as well as Real Estate Investment Trusts and Special Purpose Vehicles. There are tax matters of varying complexity, where the specific facts have a material impact on the taxpayer. As such, the complexity and individuality of tax matters is beyond the scope of this book.

regarding profitability and cash-flow, they are not alone. There are many lenders (both IMBs *and* financial institutions) that have difficulty accurately and quickly reporting profit and cash flow to the company, channel, region, and branch level. I'll leave the details in the confessional but suffice it to say that profitability and cash flow reporting (and forecasting) are not the strong suit of many lenders. Martin Kerr of Loan Vision, Nathan Burch of Vellum, Jim MacLeod of Coastal States, and other mavericks expressed amazement (as do I) at how otherwise sophisticated lenders have difficulties in these areas.

Running a lender without timely and accurate financial reporting is like flying an aircraft in the clouds without instruments. Both the lender and the aircraft are at substantial risk without timely and accurate data regarding position, speed and altitude. If a self-analysis of your company finds profitability and cash flow reporting and forecasting lacking, it's an area that can be improved reasonably quickly. The first question is 'do I have a capable CFO'? The second question is 'are my systems (LOS, hedge provider, general ledger) set up to provide the detail'? Accounting, finance and cash flow is not rocket science. A capable CFO and appropriate system configuration are straightforward matters.

Profit Metrics

Several CEOs expressed their profit goals as a threshold for adequate return. For example, a CEO of a high performing mortgage banker said, "100 basis points+ of pretax return is the target for my origination business. That's my hurdle rate for determining business decisions." Interestingly, the CEO has achieved that target four years running. That laser focus transcended volume, but it did not transcend customer experience. "We focus on our desired customer segments and deliver on our promised customer experience. My entire team is aligned with the desired experience, and our focus customer segments. Our model works. Sometimes volume is higher, sometimes lower, but we manage for 100 basis points plus." This CEO is intently dialed into the value chain that we'll discuss in a moment.

But first let's consider $1 billion in production for a moment. This is a hypothetical chart of four product types, each with $1 billion of production. Each amount is directionally accurate, but not intended to be precise. This chart is a summary snapshot of the financial elements of the value chain. Originator compensation and operational labor are held at a constant unit rate for simplicity. Jim MacLeod noted that "lenders need to focus on segments, not the market as a whole. Focus on profit, not volume." The take-away is different products have meaningfully different gross margins, with gross margin defined as revenue less direct costs of origination and operations but excluding overhead. For illustrative purposes, the chart below shows the extreme—what gross margin would be if one originated just a single product set. The following page shows an example of how a lender might target a specific gross margin strategy.

	JUMBO	HIGH BALANCE	CONVENTIONAL	GOVVIE
Annual Production	1,000,000,000	1,000,000,000	1,000,000,000	1,000,000,000
Average Loan Balance	$ 750,000	$ 550,000	$250,000	$175,000
Units	1,333	1,818	4,000	5,714
Gain on Sale, Net Margin	2.500%	2.250%	3.450%	4.500%
Gain on Sale	$25,000,000	$22,500,000	$34,500,000	$45,000,000
Originator Comp and Benefits	$11,000,000	$11,000,000	$11,000,000	$11,000,000
Pricing Concessions	$1,000,000	$1,250,000	$750,000	$200,000
Direct Labor Operational Cost	$3,466,667	$4,727,273	$10,400,000	$14,857,143
Gross Margin	*$9,533,333*	*$5,522,727*	*$12,350,000*	*$18,942,857*

For instance, if a lender wanted a high degree of FHA and VA loans, the lender may focus on geographies that have a high concentration of FHA and VA business opportunities. Working on the operational cost side, underwriters are more costly in major coastal metro areas, versus other smaller cities. I've had numerous discussions on locating operations centers in lower cost geographies, and the numbers speak for themselves. One California based lender was amazed of the cost impact of expanding its operational functions into a mid-west city. "Skilled operational labor is 30-45% less costly, and I don't have to worry about underwriters and other skilled operational people moving around every six months looking for more money as they do in California." These financial decisions regarding base level costs matter, as do operational efficiency and product mix.

I'm not aware of any mortgage banker that failed because of lack of volume. Failure of independent mortgage bankers is often a function of lack of profit and liquidity, not volume. Depository lenders seem to get in trouble from too much volume that doesn't translate into profitable operations. Post financial crisis, it's hard to fail a bank[50] due to mortgage banking activities, as regulators intervene and force remediation or a merger.

So, our discussion of financial performance starts with "what's really important?" While volume seems to be viewed as a solution to profitability, the fact base often suggests otherwise. I've organized this chapter into two sections. The first is a data-driven review of performance of the industry from 2012 to 2016, using MBA Annual Mortgage Banking Profitability Reporting.

Careful study of the loan data can lead to some very interesting insights. According to Rob Peterson, "It is evident that most LOS's have the ability to hold and retain a large of amount data and there are software solutions to provide 'business intelligence' on the data, but what sets the mavericks apart? It's the usage of that data - it's how the data is interpreted and questioned to continually drive data integrity and process improvement." The second part proposes a financial model to promote increased visibility of profit and cash flow to manage a lender's business to achieve 100 basis points of pre-tax or more.

---

[50] Many banks were seized by the FDIC in 2008 due mainly to unsafe and unsound lending practices. WaMu, IndyMac, Downey and others come to mind. There were many others in 2008-2009. During 2014, Vantage Point Bank and Millennium Bank, both largely mortgage bankers in bank charters, failed. Similarly, Proficio and Guaranty Bank failed in 2017. This is not an exhaustive list but are examples. The FDIC and OCC publicly post enforcement orders regarding all banks under formal enforcement proceedings, and one can review the issues at the above-mentioned banks and form their own conclusions. Enforcement orders for banks that operate large mortgage banking operations are public documents and are instructive of 'what not to do'. There are common themes, and adequate reporting of mortgage banking operational activities and profitability are among the themes.

A look at 2012-2016

The period 2012-2016 will go down as one of the better periods for mortgage bankers. The financial crisis of 2007-2010 was behind us. Warehouse availability was outstanding. Funded loans had very high credit quality metrics. All in, loan performance of the 2012-2016 vintages appeared very strong.

The Mortgage Bankers Association publishes a quarterly detailed report setting out aggregated data for several hundred lenders. This data is very powerful for benchmarking and for understanding the intersection between strategy and profit. We'll examine a variety of summary mortgage banking metrics in the following pages. We've divided the metrics into type of lender. "Banks" include commercial banks and thrifts engaged in mortgage banking directly or through a subsidiary. "Independent Mortgage Bankers" are non-depository lenders engaged primarily in mortgage banking activities and are owned either publicly or by private shareholders. "Other" includes subsidiaries of non-depository institutions; hedge funds or hedge fund subsidiaries and REITs.

Some performance factors over the past five years haven't changed much. The ratio of loans completed versus loans started (pull through) is one of them. The following chart shows pull through by year, by type of lender. Thus, the costs incurred in originating loans hasn't been affected by increases in fallout[51], meaning working on loans that never close. Higher fallout adversely affects productivity. The key metric missing in the statistics below is "pull through with price/fee concessions" and "pull through without price/fee concessions".

---

[51] 'Fallout' is the difference between loans started and loans actually closed. Fallout can be an absolute number, or can be expressed as a ratio, generally computed by dividing the loan units started but never closed by loan units started.

That data isn't available from MBA statistics, but it's very important as concessions represent reduced profitability on a loan.

Some observers attribute higher recent pull through in banks due to the availability of portfolio loan products, especially jumbos as well as the propensity for depository lenders to express a wider credit box for Community Reinvestment Act eligible loans. In any event, loans that don't close are a very real cost that needs to be managed. These pull through statistics are from Application to Closing. The statistics do not consider personnel and other costs spent on leads that never make an application.

PULL-THROUGH VERSUS FALL-OUT RATES
(by Lender Type)

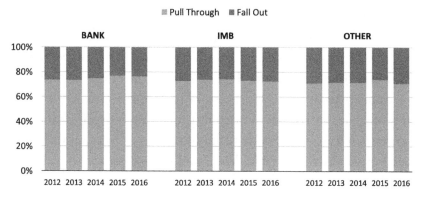

Source: MBA Mortgage Bankers Performance Report

Next, let's look at employee productivity, since we know pull through has remained relatively constant. The average lender has increased employment by 73% from 2012 to 2016, but lender loan volume by units has grown by 45%. Thus, there appears to be a productivity gap that is pushing cost to produce upward. As many CEOs interviewed have noted, there are a lot more "checkers checking the checkers"; thus a large productivity gap over the last five years.

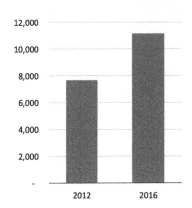

AVERAGE TOTAL LOAN UNITS

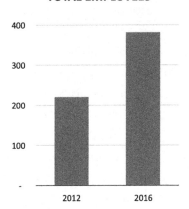

TOTAL EMPLOYEES

Source: MBA Mortgage Bankers Performance Report

As questioned earlier, does loan volume lead to profitability? A certain level of volume is, of course, necessary to achieve sufficient economies of scale and offset some of the reduced productivity caused by substantially increased regulatory costs noted above. Some may believe that annual production in the range of $500 million appears to be the level necessary to support sufficient economies of scale. In fact, as set out in the accompanying chart that follows, lenders with less than $200 million of originations have been consistently profitable. Volume does not equate to profit. A given lender's $1 billion in originations may or may not be profitable. In fact, in any given quarter over the past five years, 10-20% of the reporting lenders were not profitable. Rather than pursuing this steadfast dedication to volume, lenders should, instead, focus on maximizing profit.

The chart that follows depicts pre-tax profit by lender size, expressed as basis points of loan volume. The data suggests lenders of almost any size can be profitable. It also suggests that the strategy—loan product, channel and operational construct—is more predictive of profit than pure volume. The largest lenders had the highest profit in only one of the five years. Channel mix, geography etc. can affect profit. Large volume does not necessarily mean large profit.

PRE- TAX PROFIT (BPS) BY LENDER SIZE

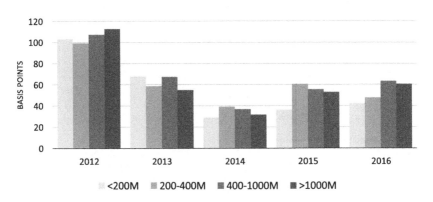

Source: MBA Mortgage Bankers Performance Report

Are there efficiencies with larger lenders, looking at average closing per production and fulfillment employees? The answer is a qualified yes, though the results may include the impact of more efficient consumer direct channels in the larger lenders that are combined with traditional retail. The distribution of monthly closing by sales employee in recent years is not significantly different by lender. Recall 2012 experienced significant refinance volume; the higher productivity of sales employees on 2012 and 2013 may have been related to servicing recapture activities of larger lenders, as well as direct to consumer refinance activities skewing results in 2012 and 2013. As volume is more purchase-oriented, the productivity differences do not appear as material. Nonetheless it is clear that productivity has declined substantially since 2012, and the borrower is bearing these costs.

MONTHLY CLOSINGS PER SALES EMPLOYEE

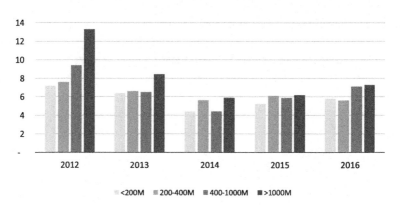

Source: MBA Mortgage Bankers Performance Report

MONTHLY CLOSINGS PER FULFILLMENT EMPLOYEE

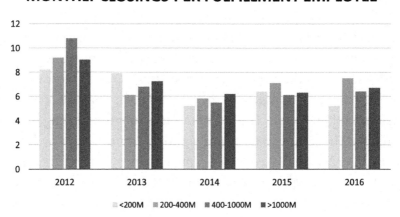

Source: MBA Mortgage Bankers Performance Report

MONTHLY CLOSING PER TOTAL PRODUCTION EMPLOYEE

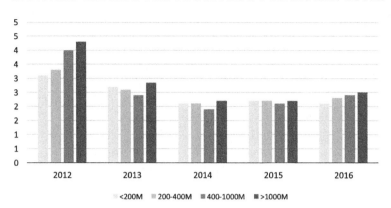

Source: MBA Mortgage Bankers Performance Report

Many lenders in our business suggest technology spend is a major component of their operational costs. The facts do not necessarily support this thesis. Personnel costs still top 200 basis points of cost, or more. Does technology spending constitute a major spend component for lenders? The following is a graph of technology spend by type of lender over time. Technology spend is a relatively small component of the cost of origination, less than 2–3% of total loan revenue. This equates to 5–7 basis points of cost per loan. Does this mean lenders are underinvesting in technology? I believe so, since the labor content of the total cost remains so high.

TECHNOLOGY SPEND (IN BPS) BY LENDER TYPE

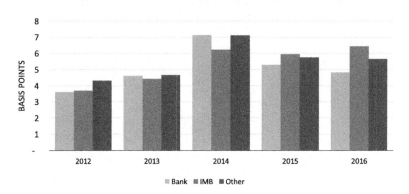

Source: MBA Mortgage Bankers Performance Report

The next area to consider is channel of origination. The chart below compares profitability for each channel: predominantly retail, a mix of retail and wholesale, and predominantly wholesale.

PROFIT (IN BPS) BY CHANNEL MIX

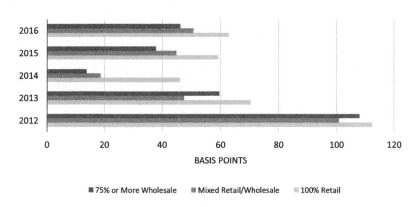

Source: MBA Mortgage Bankers Performance Report

Interestingly, the channel mix for all periods was profitable. The retail channel is generally the most profitable and includes consumer direct. Consumer direct is not separated from traditional retail, so it is not clear whether the retail is lifted by the generally much higher profitability of consumer direct business. What is also clear is that the increasing costs of origination noted above are being passed onto the consumer. Over the course of that past six years, loan origination activity has produced about 50 basis points of pretax profit, despite the reduction in productivity noted above.

This leads to several conclusions: First, the cost of regulation is very real, and contrary to the public comments by high profile regulators, the consumer is paying a lot of money for the so-called consumer protections promulgated by a variety of federal and state regulators. All lenders are subject to the increased regulatory cost load, and it is simply passed on. Second, the reduced productivity *coupled with* relatively low technology spend suggests substantial productivity increases are possible. Third, the lenders that quickly achieve substantial productivity increases will see *most of the productivity fall right to the bottom line. Lenders that achieve substantial productivity increases may not have the margin pressure simply because the industry is relatively inefficient.* If a lender becomes much more efficient than most competitors, the reduced costs drop right to the bottom line.

This is evident for a variety of reasons mentioned above, as well as because the GSEs have not differentiated guarantee fees based on volume as they had pre-crisis. The playing field is level right now regarding GSEs. Dave Stevens of the MBA cites increased competition and a level playing field access to GSEs as key elements of GSE reform. MBA wants to ensure the GSEs don't revert to the guarantee fee disparity of times past.

Next question: Does product mix affect profitability? The chart below sets out profitability by Government Loans and Conventional loans. These two loan types account for 95% of the volume of originations in the relevant years.[52] The gross revenue by loan type varies, but clearly lenders that concentrate on GSE conventional lending have lower revenues and significantly lower profitability. That effect is particularly evident in the several quarters as set out below. This is a real-world illustration of the first chart that illustrated relative profitability by loan mix.

PROFIT (IN BPS) BY LOAN TYPE MIX

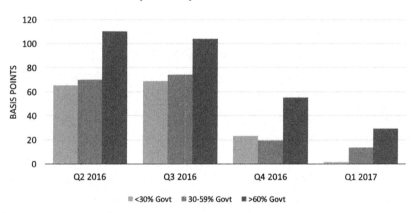

Source: MBA Mortgage Bankers Performance Report

So, in summary, a few take-aways:

- Size of the lender does not matter as much as other factors, such as efficiency, product mix and channel.

---

[52] Prior to Q2 2016, the MBA did not track loan type mix. After Q1 2017, the MBA tracked loan type mix by 50/50 buckets versus the buckets shown above.

- All the information cited above are averages among hundreds of lenders. Actual lender data varies considerably. For instance, in any given period 10-20 percent of lenders report that they were unprofitable for a given quarter.

- Productivity increases appear to offer lenders the opportunity to achieve substantial increases in profitability. Productivity increases include both the sales and fulfillment areas.

- More significantly, though, is the simple fact that volume does not equate to profit. Any given $1 billion in originations may or may not be profitable. Rather than pursuing this steadfast dedication to volume, lenders should, instead, focus on profit per loan.

- Laser focus on the value chain can drive origination pre-tax profits to 100+ basis points.

The Way Forward

The following chart represents MBA's forecast of loan production going forward. Refinance transactions continue to diminish while purchase volume accelerates. Lenders who are successful in gaining purchase market share will prosper.

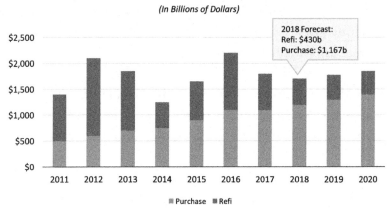

MORTGAGE ORIGINATIONS
(In Billions of Dollars)

2018 Forecast:
Refi: $430b
Purchase: $1,167b

■ Purchase ■ Refi

Source: MBA Mortgage Bankers Performance Report

The early chapters of this book focused on culture, customer experience, and customer satisfaction. The remainder of this chapter links how lenders may use the value chain concept to manage their business. Below is a conceptual model for managing the value chain, with its revenue and expense components interposed within the culture and experience dimensions of the value chain.

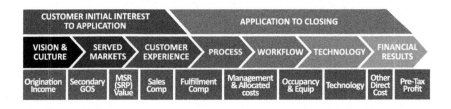

The Customer Initial Interest to Application phase is largely driven by Vision, Culture, Served Market Selection and the desired Customer Experience. This is market positioning – it's the look and feel of a lender.

If the lender's positioning and value proposition is attractive to a prospective customer, the customer makes an application, completing the revenue portion of the sale. At this point, the loan application is priced, fees are set, and servicing value and gain on sale are fixed. It's very likely that this is the best that the revenue stream is going to get with this customer, due to a variety of consumer protection laws and regulations.

Said another way, if everything is well-managed and occurs according to plan, the revenue side of the loan will be realized. (Hedging may augment the economic value of the loan, but these activities are purely financial gains unrelated to customer service.)

The Application to Closing path is where the Customer Experience is confirmed or altered. It's also where the anticipated profit is ultimately earned or leaked away. Process, Workflow, and Technology shepherds the loan from Application through Closing. The experience continues through loan boarding and servicing over time, but we'll stop at closing for the loan origination value chain analysis for now. The Application to Closing is also where much profit is lost.

What I have seen in many lenders is that an analysis of expected profitability along the value chain at consumer lock, compared to realized profitability at investor funding, has many revenue and profit leakage points[53]. A loan-level examination of profit from consumer lock to funding is a very effective data discovery project. One can see 10, 20, 30, 50 basis points of profit lost along the way. If you haven't reconciled expected profitability at the loan level to actual loan funding by an investor, you are likely missing a rich

---

[53] For a more detailed look at revenue leakage, consider an article by the author titled "Stop Leaking Revenue" in the March 2015 edition of Mortgage Banking magazine.

source for finding and plugging these leaks. Lenders that make 100+ basis points have a materially lower level of leaks, compared to less profitable peers.

Let's examine the value chain more closely using 2016 peer data for a generic IMB peer. The peer data is horizontal, in the same direction of the value chain for comparison purposes.

Origination Income	Secondary GOS	MSR (SRP) Value	Sales Comp	Fulfillment Comp	Management & Allocated costs	Occupancy & Equip	Technology	Other Direct Cost	Pre-Tax Profit
75	205	98	141	54	37	16	6	68	55
378 BASIS POINTS				*323 BASIS POINTS*					

By definition, Origination Income includes fees retained by the lender and not passed on to third parties; Gain on Sale is net of hedge costs and gains; MSR value is the value of Mortgage Servicing Rights if retained or the Servicing Release Premium ("SRP") if sold; Sales compensation includes commissions, benefits, salaries, overrides and bonuses for originators, sales assistants and origination management; Fulfillment compensation includes operational costs of closing a loan including compensation, benefits and bonuses for operational and operations management; Management includes senior management and allocated costs such as corporate overhead; Technology includes LOS and other technology costs excluding compensation; Other Direct Costs includes secondary, post-closing, quality control ("QC") and non-recovered third party costs.

Consider benchmarking your own results against these 2016 statistics for additional insights into your lending results.

Using this model, we can then analyze the revenue and expense stack of a variety of operating options. For example, we can look at Bank, IMB, and Other lender groups by component of revenue or cost. The relative cost of sales compensation can be seen as the major driver of cost base by lender type.

REVENUE/EXPENSES (IN BPS) BY LENDER TYPE

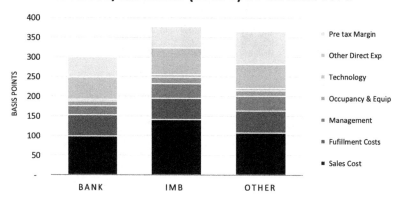

Source: MBA Mortgage Bankers Performance Report

Loan size also drives performance. Consider that loan size is both geographically driven as well as driven by loan type. FHA loans are generally smaller than conventional ones and carry higher margins. The impact of loan type and geography appear interrelated on the loan size graph below. Compensation for operational elements declines by loan size as expected. Larger loans do not experience a commensurate increase in effort from operational employees. In some cases, it might be argued larger conventional loans require less effort, as the credit box of GSE loan vintages in recent years are very tight, so the expected operational effort would be lower.

REVENUE/EXPENSES (IN BPS) BY LOAN SIZE

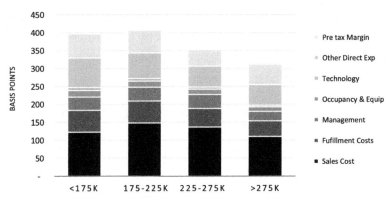

Source: MBA Mortgage Bankers Performance Report

The results by lender size suggest that each lender group has a revenue and cost structure that supports the model. Notable among smaller lenders is sales compensation. This factor may be due to self-production of loans by ownership, with compensation being realized as profitability as opposed to sales commission. Fulfillment costs, Management costs, and Other Direct costs for larger lenders appear smaller per loan, likely the result of some economies of scale.

PRE-TAX PROFIT (BPS) BY LENDER SIZE

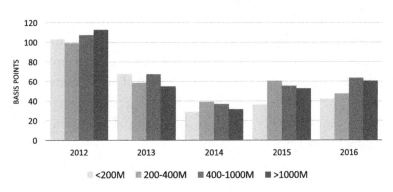

Source: MBA Mortgage Bankers Performance Report

The Revenue Stack for lender size is different, likely reflecting a pure best effort strategy for smaller lenders, with a more sophisticated hedging strategy leading to increased revenue for larger lenders. The largest lenders likely have third party channels included, which reduce both revenue and cost. All in all, it is remarkable that a small lender and a large lender are both profitable, with an 18-basis point spread in profit suggesting scale is not a driving factor in origination profit at this point in time.

Said another way, culture, strategy and customer experience seem to be the driving force of profitability, not loan volume. Larger lenders have larger absolute profitability but it is important that a smaller lender can earn an acceptable profit in the current market.

The impact of channel selection is much more apparent in the graph below. The channel breakout for consumer direct versus retail represents a small sample, so extension of these results should be cautioned. Consumer direct channels I have observed tend to have much higher profitability than the amounts listed below. The third-party origination ("TPO") wholesale channel appears representative, with lower revenue (due to broker compensation) and costs (paid by the broker) shifting the overall revenue and cost structure, but still resulting in profitable operations. In some respects, the TPO shifting of the cost structure onto brokers could represent a more easily scalable and de scalable business model as demand fluctuates.

REVENUE/EXPENSE (IN BPS) BY ORIGINATION CHANNEL

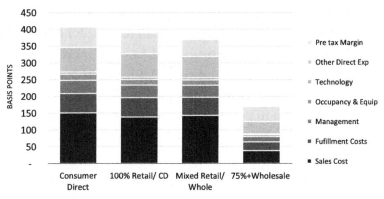

Source: MBA Mortgage Bankers Performance Report

Finally, product mix profitability is apparent by FHA/VA mix. Higher profitability is apparent in the higher FHA/VA mix. Some of the most profitable origination models are structured towards FHA/VA lending in secondary and tertiary geographies, or in consumer direct models focusing on FHA/VA product (though these operations have a higher refinance component, and it is not clear whether these models can translate into a primarily purchase driven model.) The following chart shows FHA percentage mix, such as <30%, 30-59%, and >60%:

REVENUE/EXPENSES (IN BPS) BY PRODUCT MIX

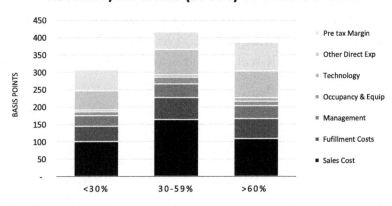

Source: MBA Mortgage Bankers Performance Report

Revenue and Profit Leakage

The prior discussion provides a glimpse into culture/strategy as it relates to profit. The data is actual data, but names, branch names, and locations are all anonymized. Think back to the overall business model, the culture, and customer experience result in a completed loan application. When the loan application is complete, the total potential revenue (except for hedge gains/losses) is fixed due to consumer protection regulations. That's the best it can be. Revenue and profit leakage may occur as the loan proceeds through the approval and closing process.

Revenue leakage occurs when the potential revenue as of loan application is not realized. It can leak for a variety of reasons: price concessions, lock extensions, changes in loan level pricing adjustments ("LLPAs") that are not captured within the lender's system, and a variety of other causes.

Profit leakage includes revenue leakage, as well as cure costs, inefficient fulfillment processes such as re-work, re-ordering of third party services, duplicative ordering of services, fulfillment errors resulting in ineligibility to the intended investor, pre-funding QC issues requiring remediation, post-closing findings other than trailing documents, investor funding stipulations, missing information that delays or reduces data integrity in loan boarding, reformation of documents, first payment exceptions, escrow exceptions… the list goes on. These are profit leakages at the loan level.

There are also profit leakages that are systemic. For instance, a loan officer who is producing less than the company average likely leaks more profit than is apparent. Look at the population of loan originators in an anonymized lender. This lender's model permits relatively low production originators to continue employment. The lender has the view that all production is good production. The lender's productivity per loan officer is low, with fulfillment productivity at slightly below average levels. The profitability result is predictable. Low originator productivity leads to elevated per loan cost to originate, which affects profitability. The lender believes volume is necessary to offset the costs of fulfillment. Unspoken is the possibility of scaling down the operation, laying off fulfillment personnel and making more absolute profit. But a large volume of high-balance conventional and jumbo pushes the lender into the bottom quartile of profitability on a consistent basis. This is a good example of "volume does not lead to profitability".

Maylin Casanueva, Chief Operating Officer of Teraverde®, and her team developed a solution to identify revenue leakage and turn it into profit intelligence. The view of closed loans for anonymized data from a lender shows the impact of loan officer churn over two quarters. Note the large number of loan originators that processed less than 20 loans in the six month period displayed on the following chart. The costs of hiring and then off-boarding loan officers had a very real impact of productivity and cost.

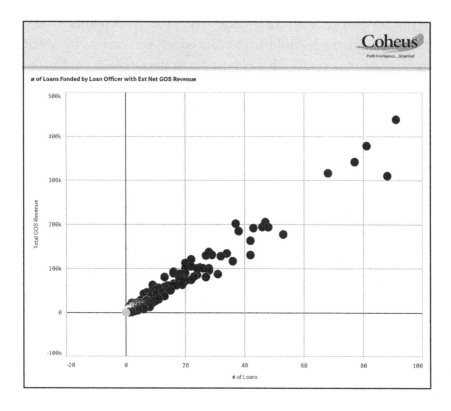

Revenue leakage can also be more insidious. A regional pricing strategy coupled with some pricing engine errors in loan level price adjusters can be seen on the next chart. Two branches produced significantly lower risk-adjusted pricing due to LLPA and branch margin errors in the pricing engine. This situation subsisted, because the relationship between FICO and rate had not been reviewed in granular detail.

This is a classic definition of systemic revenue leakage. We once assisted a client merging two lenders while migrating to a new pricing engine. We used testing scripts for various branch/product/region combinations—about 650 scripts in total. The initial error rate was in the 20% range, with the average error at 27 basis points. Undetected, these errors would have reduced lender revenue by about six basis points overall. That is pure profit degradation, and at the lender's volume would have translated to millions in profits. But six basis points of leakage would not have been obvious if one only looked at overall gain on sale.

Another lender used a profit leakage tool to compare the complete pricing estimated at pricing engine lock to the consumer, to secondary lock/hedge, to clear to close pricing, to pricing received from investor funding. The lender analyzed leakage at the LLPA level, as well as base pricing levels. The results were amazing. Leakage averaged about 28 basis points. The root causes included pricing engine mis-coding, LLPA overlay mis-coding, inconsistent recovery of LLPAs when loan terms changed, investor funding errors, as well as a variety of one-off mistakes. Not included were insufficient overlay charges for risk elements, where the lender could have increased pricing on a risk basis for higher risk loans, harvesting that profit as compensation for taking additional risks.

Branch Profitability: Here's how an issue in the pricing engine set-up was discovered in two branches. This is data discovery at its best. Looking at the factual data using an associative augmented intelligence process is remarkably effective at identifying areas of profit leakage. Profit leakage becomes profit improvement when the root cause is identified.

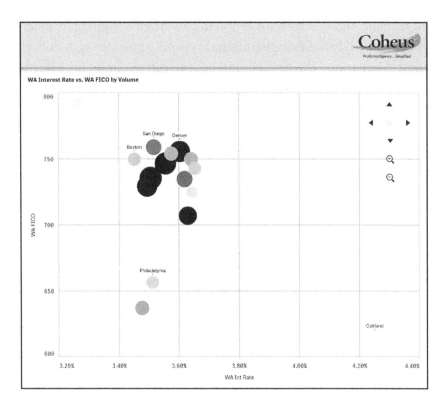

Revenue leakage, as with many issues facing the industry, stems from the double-bind of Dodd-Frank. Gain on Sale Margin among products varies considerably, but Dodd-Frank prohibits compensation based on loan terms. This is a key dichotomy of profit management post Dodd-Frank. This dichotomy is amplified as originator compensation is often tied to volume, not profit. Originators tend to pursue higher balance lower margin loans, since their compensation cannot be legally tied to loan type. Some loan originators also may manipulate the compensation rules, since they know they cannot be held accountable to pay for errors.

Loan Officer Level Profitability: One can see this easily with an analysis of profit by originator. How does one do that? Aggregate all revenue and fees by loan originator by month. Aggregate compensation paid to the originator and compute gross margin dollars from origination. The profitability by loan officer shows not all volume is good volume. This exercise can be done in real time with the right profit intelligence solution.

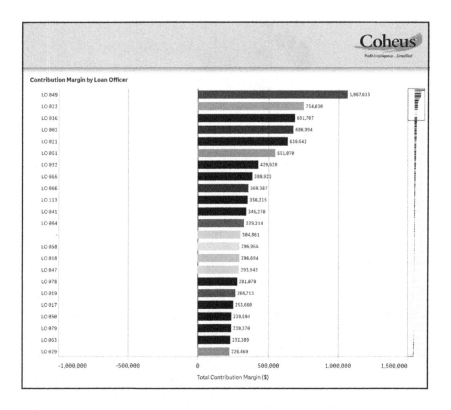

Concessions: We compared pull-through for a lender based on pull-through without concessions and pull-through with concessions. The anonymized data below isolates a cohort of originators by pull-through and by concessions. Surprisingly, high pull through is not always the best measure of loan officer success. Net pretax profits from two loan officers with 80% pull through are compared below. A low level of concession produced the most pretax profit of $92,000. Surprisingly, 80% pull through with a high level of concessions was about as profitable as a 65% pull through with low concessions (both about $75,000). 65% pull through with high concession was worst at $62,000. The takeaway is that pull through and price concessions materially affect profitability. A clear source of profit leakage was highlighted, *if* the lender can isolate price concessions by loan officer.

LOAN OFFICER	#1	#2	#3	#4
LOAN VOLUME	$20M	$20M	$20M	$20M
PULL THROUGH	80%	65%	80%	65%
PULL THROUGH ADJUSTED LOAN VOLUME	$16M	$13M	$16M	$13M
AVERAGE PRETAX MARGIN CONSTANT (BPS)	60	60	60	60
# OF LOANS W/ CONCESSIONS (AT 25BPS)	50	10	10	50
ADJUSTED PRETAX MARGIN	47.5	57.5	57.5	47.5
PRETAX MARGIN	$76K	$74.75K	$92K	$61.75K

Another source of profit leakage is compliance cure costs. Interestingly, cure costs are not ratably distributed by operational and origination employee, or by source. The following chart illustrates a variety of cure costs, some more difficult to resolve than others. The takeaway from this chart is that a lender's "zero tolerance fee cure costs" arise because of errors by the lender *in disclosing their own fees*. And in a few cases, non-curable fee tolerance issues created $38,000 in scratch and dent losses. This is an easy to correct situation that eliminates $142,000 of cure costs by correcting lender fee disclosure errors.

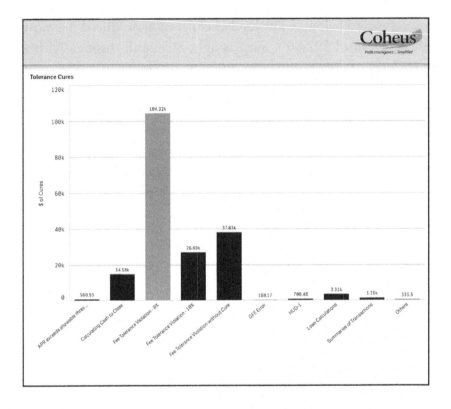

Employee Productivity: Fulfillment employee productivity may also be variable. The following charts show processor and underwriter turnaround time and productivity. One can see significant standard deviation in the results. We spoke of standard deviation in chapter one, regarding temperatures in Florida versus Death Valley, CA. The average was the same, but the standard deviation was wide. Same observation here. A process that is tightly defined and well-executed should have a low standard deviation.

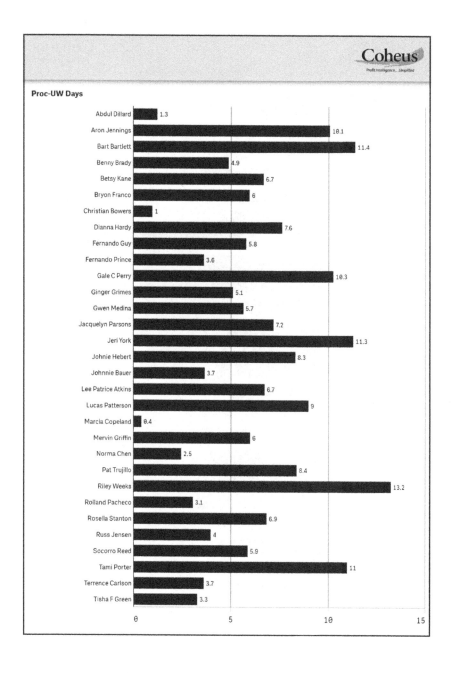

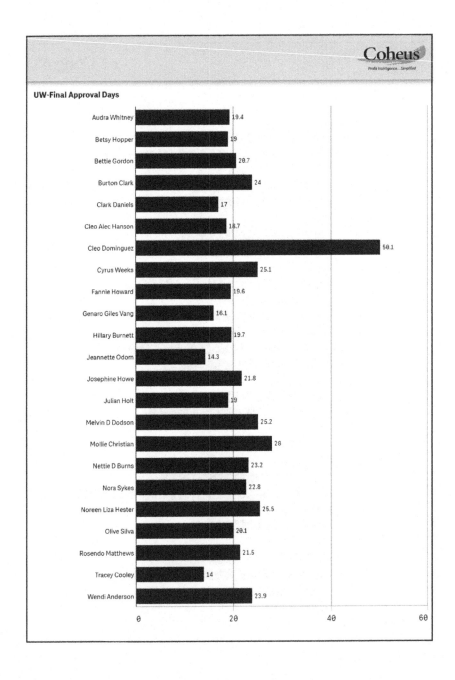

UW-Final Approval Days

The same is true for turnaround times. There are significant standard deviations among branches and operational employees.

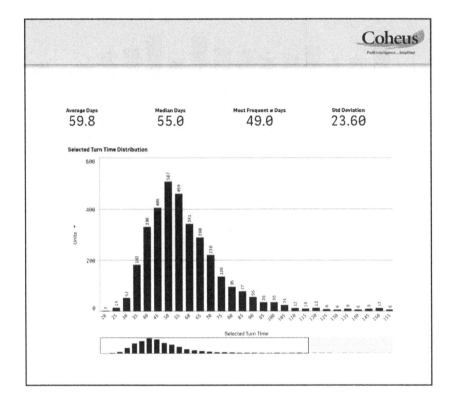

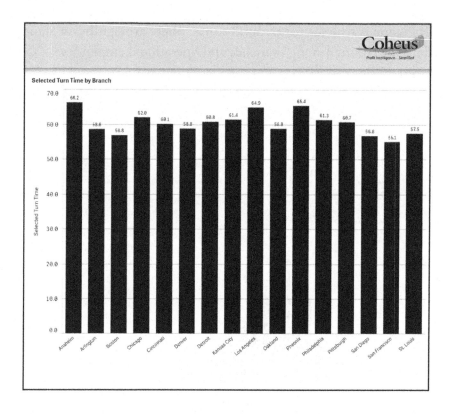

One can also determine the speediest path through the lending process. Some loan officers and fulfillment personnel function as faster combinations than others. It's worthwhile it to study the combinations to uncover those that are fastest, find out why, and spread the techniques. The same goes with the slowest. Again, find out why and correct the technique. Here is the slowest combination from our anonymized dataset:

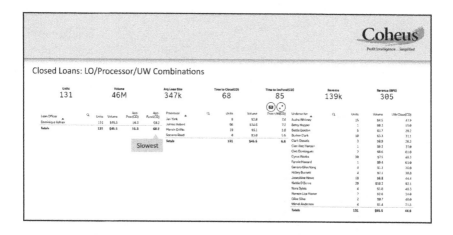

Dwell time on the warehouse line has a direct correlation to hedge costs and interest costs. The faster a loan can fund with the investor, the higher the profitability. The hedge vehicle may be reset or reused if a loan funds quickly. Warehouse times vary and measuring dwell time is important by investor and warehouse lender. Slow turn times by an investor may negate a pricing advantage. For example, if a loan can fund in two days versus 20, the pickup is 18 basis points of hedge cost, about one basis point a day. That speed can price through 12.5 basis points of apparent advantage in execution!

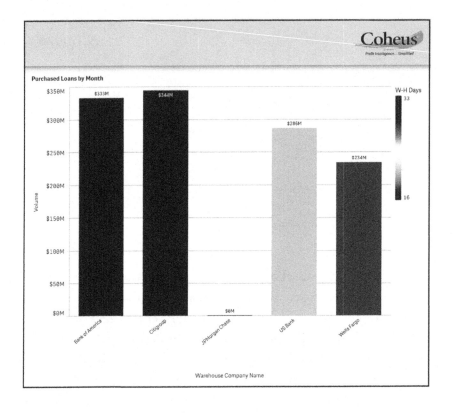

Finally, pre-funding QC can shed light on the overall processes of the lender. It's educational to track error rates among loan officers, processors, underwriters, closers and appraisers. Find the best and spread the techniques. Find the worst and remediate the issues. The following charts show two graphs of error rates by employee.

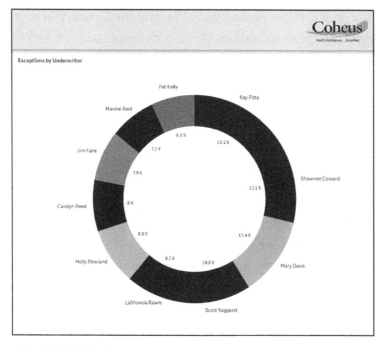

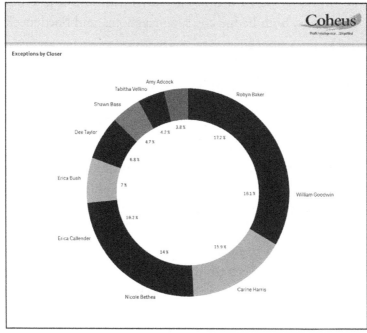

The list goes on, but profit leakage occurs for a variety of reasons. Excessive hedge costs, fallout costs, concession costs, relocks, low originator volume, low fulfillment employee productivity, excessive investor stipulations, non-saleable loans requiring scratch and dent pricing or refinance, low lead conversion, high warehouse dwell time (both interest cost and hedge cost burn), non-economic products, employee churn, branch churn, investor churn, fulfillment end-of-month fire drills, "rush loans", prima donna syndrome, etc.

Finally, a few thoughts on moving the needle on the origination side. If it takes 62 days from application to investor funding and you want to reduce that to 50 days, where do you begin? Think about the distribution curve above and begin with the worst standard deviation segments. That's where you can make a big difference in averages and in customer satisfaction. Remember the J.D. Power survey? Take longer than promised, and customer satisfaction plummets. Long turn times usually mean re-work, re-disclosure, cure costs, high hedge costs, concessions, and bottlenecks.

Loan Servicing – Pro and Con

My introduction to servicing was in 1989. Defaults were low. The servicer collected 25 basis points of servicing fee, had the use of deposits when short term rates were 7%, and direct cost to service a loan was under $40 per loan. Life was straightforward, and servicing was a relatively simple asset.

Loan servicing used to be considered an effective offset to variations in production. When originations ebb, the servicing provides cash flow to offset the slower origination levels. And when rates fall, refinance and recapture of servicing serve as the production hedge to offset servicing run-offs. The production hedge was an added bonus. At the time, one didn't capitalize self-generated servicing, and life truly was pretty straightforward.

The FASB unwittingly sowed the seeds for volatility in mortgage servicing rights assets, and more importantly provided the fuel to generate the explosive growth of subprime mortgages. The ability to capitalize a future stream of income from subprime assets was a necessary ingredient for the growth of the segment. (High relative interest rates and excess servicing fees could be capitalized to turn individual loans into valuable assets fetching pricing of 108, 109—the sky was the limit. Add aggressive estimates on loss ratios and prepayment penalties to prevent refinances, and a perfect storm was set in motion.)

During the early 2000's, a few large correspondent lenders controlled a large segment of the servicing market. Then the crisis hit. Delinquencies increased. Strategic defaults hit the portfolio. Freddie Mac and Fannie Mae imposed foreclosure moratoriums. Repurchases. Mortgage Insurance rescissions. Jingle mail (when the homeowner sends in the keys). HAMP. HARP. Judicial foreclosures grind to a halt. Then the regulators and plaintiff attorneys come at you. Then the gift that keeps on giving: the CFPB. Maybe servicing isn't such a great idea? Several large banks significantly reduced holdings of servicing post-2010.

Let's examine the question of scale in servicing. Is large scale required for profitability in servicing? The answer is not so much if one has high quality servicing from a credit perspective. Servicing with low delinquency can be profitable from low to high volume, as the accompanying chart demonstrates. Can the lender afford the investment of cash into mortgage servicing rights? The question of servicing retention is one of operational strategy and cash flow. Surprisingly, servicing scale is not necessarily a driver of profitability.

BASIS POINTS	<2,500	2,500-10,000	10,000-50,000	>50,000	TOTAL
DIRECT REVENUE					
Servicing Fees	26.39	26.58	26.80	28.89	27.08
First Mortgages, Seconds, Other	25.56	25.30	25.32	22.52	24.78
Subservicing Fees Earned	0.84	1.28	1.48	6.37	2.30
Late Fees and Other Ancillary Income	0.88	1.93	3.38	4.40	2.57
Total Direct Servicing Revenue	**27.27**	**28.51**	**30.18**	**33.29**	**29.65**
DIRECT EXPENSES					
Personnel	6.89	4.89	5.08	6.61	5.86
Loan Administrative Employees	6.37	4.17	4.24	5.58	5.10
Benefits	0.51	0.54	0.65	0.85	0.63
Other Personnel Expense	0.01	0.18	0.20	0.18	0.14
Occupancy and Equipment	0.15	0.35	0.60	0.60	0.42
Other Direct Expenses	7.79	6.91	8.36	6.15	7.39
Subservicing Fees Paid	7.36	5.24	6.16	2.69	5.53
Other Miscellaneous Expenses	0.43	1.67	2.19	3.46	1.85
Total Direct Expenses	**14.82**	**12.15**	**14.04**	**13.36**	**13.67**
DIRECT SERVICING NET INCOME	**12.45**	**16.36**	**16.14**	**19.92**	**15.98**
INDIRECT EXPENSES					
Unreimbursed FC/REO Svg Expenses	0.02	0.33	0.44	1.09	0.44
Corporate Allocation	1.65	0.94	1.99	2.89	1.84
Total Indirect Expenses	**1.67**	**1.28**	**2.44**	**3.97**	**2.28**
NET INTEREST INCOME					
Escrow Earnings	-	0.01	0.10	0.16	0.06
Corporate Interest Losses on MBS Pools	-	(0.37)	(0.13)	(0.29)	(0.18)
Other Interest Expense	(0.06)	(0.11)	(0.30)	(1.59)	(0.46)
Net Interest Income	**(0.06)**	**(0.47)**	**(0.33)**	**(1.72)**	**(0.59)**
NET OPERATING INCOME	**10.72**	**14.61**	**13.37**	**14.23**	**13.12**

Does credit quality really control servicing profitability? Performing loan servicing is thought to be relatively easy. That may be true if ease of servicing is confined to collection of payments as set out above.

However, servicing regulatory risk is very high and increasing, even for performing loans. Escrow analysis, satisfaction management, natural disaster impact, consumer confusion, and misunderstanding contribute to regulatory risk. So, credit quality is just one dimension of servicing profitability.

Default servicing (loans that are not performing as agreed) has become exponentially more difficult due to the proliferation of federal and state servicing guidelines. Slow foreclosure actions in judicial foreclosure states, activist attorneys general, and class action litigators add to economic and reputation risk.

Investment in servicing by a mortgage banker consumes cash. The costs associated with originating and closing the loan are incurred upfront, but the cash flow from servicing occurs over time. This means the investment in MSRs must be made by the lender, usually out of the lender's capital base. This is particularly important for IMBs since capital is necessary to expand the business and MSRs compete for that scarce capital.

Banks have more liquidity to finance MSRs but are subject to a capital haircut for MSRs exceeding a threshold. So, in a perverse way, regulations (Basel III in particular) insert a perverse incentive for banks to limit MSRs although banks have the most access to liquidity as well as potential natural servicing prepayment risk hedges elsewhere on their balance sheets.

Prepayment risk is difficult to hedge, particularly for IMBs. Most IMBs do not hedge MSRs with financial instruments, rather relying on the production hedge, servicing recapture programs, or both to minimize the economic risk of servicing.

Government National Mortgage Association (GNMA) wants all issuers to hold some servicing but is also concerned particularly with IMB liquidity and capital levels. GNMA servicing holds some specific risks not present in other types of servicing, particularly regarding the formulaic requirements of default servicing. If a particular portfolio has a high default level, then the lender is required to make significant principal, interest, tax and insurance (PITI) advances. Loans may be situated in judicial foreclosure states, where foreclosure times are extended. Lenders must advance PITI on loans that are delinquent or in foreclosure. Loans in judicial states requiring advances of 24–48 months on PITI are not uncommon. In cases where the loans involved lender credit, or were made in higher interest rate environments, the recovery of the interest advances due to differences in the note rate and debenture rate can be material. Lender advances are not always fully recoverable even when loans are serviced perfectly. During this period, the servicing fee is not being collected, either. Servicing can consume a considerable amount of cash in these circumstances.

Servicing errors regarding timeliness of foreclosure and loss mitigation activity can be very costly. A case in point: a GNMA servicer utilized a subservicer to service FHA loans. The particular portfolio had a high default level, which required the lender to make significant principal, interest, tax, and insurance advances. The subservicer, at the servicer's request, was slightly lenient on foreclosure timeframes resulting in curtailment of interest advanced, due to missing the first legal date for foreclosure. In aggregate, the losses from non-reimbursement of interest advances were significant.

Cash Flow and Liquidity

Cash flow and liquidity are the keys to successful mortgage banking. Without cash and liquidity, options, and indeed viability are severely reduced. What are the various cash cycles in mortgage banking? The monthly origination cash cycle, servicing cycle, Mortgage Servicing Rights cash cycle, default and foreclosure cash cycles? Pipeline growth and hedging cash cycles?

The Ebb and Flow of Cash Flow

Mortgage Banking inherently consumes cash during the origination process. The chart below shows the hypothetical sources and uses of cash for a single loan originated via a retail channel with *servicing retained*, versus accrual profitability. This example is simplified and makes assumptions to illustrate the cash flow process. The amounts are in basis points:

DAYS FROM START OF CONSUMER INTEREST IN A LOAN	10	45	55	70	YEAR 1	
PHASE OF LOAN IN PROCESS	CONSUMER INTEREST	LOAN APPLICATION	LOAN WORKFLOW MANAGEMENT	CONSUMER LOAN CLOSING	INVESTOR FUNDING	CAPITALIZED MORTGAGE SERVICING RIGHTS	TOTAL
REVENUE		20	-	-	275	90	385
COST	20	-	80	200	40	-	340
CUMULATIVE NET PRE-TAX PROFIT	(20)	-	(80)	(280)	(45)	45	45
CUMULATIVE NET CASH FLOW	(20)	-	(80)	(280)	(45)	(45)	(45)

The process starts with initial interest from a consumer. This initial interest could result from purchased lead, a response to a website or social media, or a borrower identified by a loan officer. From initial consumer interest through application, about 20 basis points are expended for leads, marketing, credit reports, and associated costs of the infrastructure.

At loan application the borrower is assumed to pay an application fee in addition to third party fees, bringing the net cash back to neutral. This is assumed to occur on the 10th day after initial consumer interest.

Once the application is underway, labor for various operational activities and associated third party costs are incurred, totaling about 80 basis points. If the loan falls out, the lender is cash negative for these costs incurred.

If the loan closes, loan officer, branch, and related compensation and costs are paid out on the 55th day. At this point, the lender is about 280 basis points cash negative. The lender then waits for loan funding by the investor, while paying shipping, post-closing, and any cure costs. At funding, the lender receives the purchase price and capitalizes the mortgage servicing asset, bringing the lender to a cash positive position of 45 basis points about 70 days after initial consumer interest.

When the lender is building a pipeline of loans (as in the Spring homebuying season or when interest rates fall, and refinance activity grows), the growth of the pipeline uses cash. When a lender's pipeline is falling (when home buying season is over, or rates increase reducing refinancing) the cash position of the lender improves. Note that cash flow and reported earnings are different.

In the discussion above, retained servicing means the lender will capitalize Mortgage Servicing Rights (MSRs) of 90 basis points, and record the profit from capitalization. But the lender will not have the cash in hand. Rather, the capitalized MSRs will be financed out of the lender's capital.

The Impact

Bearing the burden of the complexities of the cash flow process does not fall evenly across the industry. Since Independent Mortgage Bankers (IMBs) have the MSR assets but not the cash from a servicing sale, they feel the impact of this ebb and flow much more than banks.

So, let's recap the cash flow matters. Lenders must finance the costs on each loan from consumer interest through investor funding. Loan fallout consumes cash which is never recovered. Lenders holding servicing must finance the MSRs over a 3 to 6 year period during which reported profit exceeds actual cash flow.

Retained servicing gets more complex when defaults exceed minimal levels. A lender must advance principal and interest as well as taxes and insurance when a borrower is in default. Loans with high default tendencies (think FHA) can consume lender cash, especially when collateral is located in judicial foreclosure states.

No discussion of cash flow would be complete without re-emphasizing revenue leakage. We discussed profit leakage above and didn't really hammer home the cash flow impact. But, revenue leakage is a cash loss that can affect a lender's liquidity. The sources of revenue leakage are varied and many. They include:

- uncollectable fees and repricings;

- cures for disclosure defects;

- price concessions on rate locks, float downs, and relocks;

- consumer concessions for goodwill;

- rework of loans due to workflow and business process defects;

- lock extensions required for investor funding stipulations not cured on a timely basis;

- unwillingness for an investor to fund a loan due to document defects, alleged underwriting or compliance defects, etc.;

- guarantees and advances to loan officers and branches that fall short of projections;

- errors in servicing, resulting in unrecoverable interest advances and other corporate advances;

- loss mitigation costs for retained servicing that are not recoverable; and

- litigation and regulatory enforcement costs for process, disclosure and other issues.

The list could go on and on, really. What may help to illustrate how varied the complexities involved are is to walk through some real-life examples. In one scenario, a lender's pricing engine had errors in branch margin and loan level price adjusters. The result? Two million dollars in revenue leakage.

A lender concentrated on pull-through—and not pull-through after price concession—resulting in a whopping $7 million in revenue leakage. Yet another lender did not recognize that margins on conforming high balance loans that exceeded TBA tolerance for MBS were resulting in 50-90 basis point of profit reduction on high balance loans. The lender had recruited several branches that focused on high balance conforming lending. You can imagine the result there.

Poor operating procedures and servicing practices are often at fault as well. One servicer with master mortgage insurance (MI) policy violations was hit with a jaw-dropping $100 million in MI rescissions and penalties. In another scenario, the Federal Deposit Insurance Corporation (FDIC) and Department of Justice (DOJ) ended up alleging disparate impact against a firm when poor pricing engine configuration resulted in higher LLPAs for certain borrowers. This situation translated into not only millions of dollars in reimbursements but also multi-million dollar penalties. And lack of detection of revenue leakage arising from fraudulent practices in several mortgage banking "P&L branches" resulted in the failure of an FDIC insured bank.

The lessons here are clear—the basic process of mortgage banking requires sufficient liquidity and capital to fund cash usage, and constant vigilance to detect revenue and profit leakage. The rewards are 100+ basis points of pretax profit levels and positive cash flow.

So where are the thought leaders on these issues? Stan Middleman encouraged a sense of "history" in the industry. In the aftermath of the financial crisis, Stan was surprised by the depth of the correction.

"What made it awful was the evaporation of liquidity across the board." What would have ameliorated things for many, Stan believes, would have come from having a historical perception and understanding that markets don't snap back in an instant. "Some people in our business were bad historians." A whole series of regulations and laws were enacted to prevent the stress created by subprime mortgage securities.

As we began this chapter, we discussed profit, cash flow, and liquidity. In the end, cash flow and liquidity are the most important elements of mortgage banking. Again, to quote fighter pilots, "speed is life". In mortgage banking, cash flow and resulting liquidity are life. Without liquidity, a lender's life will be short indeed.

CHAPTER SIX
Information Security for Mavericks

Mavericks think about information security because lenders amass a large amount of non-public customer information in the ordinary course of business. A mortgage loan application contains a complete financial snapshot of the borrower. Income, assets, credit lines, loans, employment information, social security numbers, work history, and data on ethnicity. All this information is aggregated in a mortgage loan file, making the industry a target for bad actors. The financial services industry has been designated as one of the six critical infrastructure sectors in the United States.

Regulatory Safeguards

The "safeguards" rule of the Gramm Leach Bliley Act (GLBA) calls for lenders to utilize the best security approach that is both readily available and cost effective. This requirement applies to banks and mortgage bankers. Information Security is often the purview of the IT Department, but Information Security should be one of the key priorities of the maverick CEO. Information Security is not just about firewalls and technical systems; security is a business strategy that must be embedded throughout the mortgage banking operation. And with more solutions coming from FinTech, there are more opportunities to have data lost or misappropriated.

Mortgage bankers deploy branches and loan officers to remote locations. The Loan Origination System is a treasure trove of Personally Identifiable Information (PII). It includes credit reports, social security numbers, employment histories, and lists of assets—everything a criminal could want. In some cases, ethically impaired loan officers or branch managers might also want it.

Most LOS systems are provided as Software as a Service (SaaS), meaning the LOS provider hosts the system and provides overall system security. The lender's system administrator maintains access controls but oftentimes permits excessive system privileges due to poorly defined LOS roles and responsibilities. Excessive user privileges are often at the heart of PII loss from LOS systems.

Litigation Risk

PII loss can have significant consequences. According to HousingWire, "A California jury ordered Guaranteed Rate to pay more than $25 million in damages to a fellow mortgage lender, Mount Olympus Mortgage Company, stemming from accusations that a former employee of Mount Olympus Mortgage stole client information and loan files and took them with him when he went to work at Guaranteed Rate."

Lawyers representing Mount Olympus alleged a former licensed loan officer worked with several other former employees to illegally transfer hundreds of private consumer loan files from Mount Olympus Mortgage's computer systems to Guaranteed Rate. The loan officer allegedly stole 200 active loan files, as well as the confidential information of approximately 900 Mount Olympus Mortgage clients.

According to HousingWire, "the company filed a civil lawsuit and asserted claims against the loan officer for breach of contract, breach of fiduciary duty and fraud, and against both Guaranteed Rate and the loan officer for violations of California Penal Code, which covers the unlawful theft of computer data, as well as conversion and misappropriation of the confidential loan files…an Orange County, California jury found the defendants liable on all counts, awarding $25,100,000, including $13,000,000 for punitive damages to Mount Olympus Mortgage."[54]

Frequent litigation arises from allegedly inadequate controls over a lender's pipeline of leads and loans. The litigation often occurs when a branch office resigns, and the lender losing the branch performs a forensic review and discovers some of their data was removed in process. This happens often enough that mavericks find ways to protect themselves and their customers.

In another instance, a lender belatedly found out that a just hired top loan officer transferred the entire contents (several gigabytes) of her former employer's laptop to the new lender. This included PII and other proprietary information of the former lender. The lender intervened, destroyed the data, and severely admonished the new loan officer and the low-level IT employee that unwittingly helped

[54] https://www.housingwire.com/articles/36597-guaranteed-rate-ordered-to-pay-25m-to-mount-olympus-mortgage-for-data-theft

the loan officer. The lender then never fully trusted the loan officer, and the relationship didn't last long.

Considering these incidents, mavericks know Information Security is not just technical systems. It's the procedures used to monitor what is happening to your LOS, servicing systems, CRM systems and your data. What is being exfiltrated, and by whom? What is being imported, and by whom? What controls exist to monitor and control these processes?

Phishing and Other Social Engineering Risks

Phishing is the precursor to eighty to ninety percent of "headline" security breaches. Nathan Burch of Vellum Mortgage was hit by a CEO email compromise. A phishing email and follow-up call convinced a finance employee that a transfer of $21,000 was legitimate. After that incident, Nathan installed additional controls and ensured all of his employees completed social engineering and phishing awareness training. Importantly, he then employed continued phishing exercises to detect which employees were susceptible to social engineering schemes. Over the course of six months, susceptibility and dangerous activities such as clicking on links or opening attachments fell from about one in five employees pretraining to about one in one hundred.

Phil DeFronzo initiated social engineering training, dual authentication, and endpoint monitoring, as well as additional safeguards and controls. Several state regulators noted that Norcom's security met the requirements of their respective states, including some states that have highly elevated expectations for information security.

Mavericks know that penetration testing and information technology audits can result in a false sense of security. These types of controls rarely prevent social engineering fraud. So, what should mavericks do?

First, review a white paper titled "The Basic Components of an Information Security Program" by the Information Security Work Group of the Mortgage Bankers Association Residential Technology Forum. It's a good overview of security basics.

The next logical step is an Information Security Risk Assessment. Have a non-IT executive engage a professional firm to conduct an independent risk assessment and gap assessment from an attacker's point of view to determine the lender's current security posture and risk profile. Consider engaging an ethical hacking security provider to consider the types of physical, cultural, operational, system, and internal control breaches that innovative hackers and employees could perpetrate.

Inquire of your security team about if and how information security information is shared within security working groups organized in your industry. MBA has an Information Security Workgroup. The Financial Services Information Sharing and Analysis Center (FS-ISAC).

FS-ISAC describes its function as:

> *The only industry forum for collaboration on critical security threats facing the global financial services sector. When attacks occur, early warning and expert advice can mean the difference between business continuity and widespread business catastrophe. Members of the Financial Services*

Information Sharing and Analysis Center (FS-ISAC) worldwide receive timely notification and authoritative information specifically designed to help protect critical systems and assets from physical and cyber security threats.

Mavericks ensure their company uses a secure document management approach. Encrypted email or another secure document system is used for all customer communication involving PII.

Controlling access to your systems and networks also involves being fully aware of anyone who has access to the systems or networks. This includes vendors: Criminals sometimes attempt to get jobs on cleaning crews for the purpose of breaking into computers for the sensitive information that they expect to find there. Controlling access also includes being careful about having computer or network repair personnel working unsupervised on systems or devices. It is easy for them to steal private/sensitive information.

Companies run by mavericks usually perform deep pre-employment background and credit checks, including social media searches to identify potentially unfit employee candidates. Require written explanations of any adverse data and consider whether the explanation is credible. Monitor employee compliance carefully during the initial period after hiring to identify potential issues.

Care is to be taken with terminations of employment, both voluntary and involuntary. End of employment should result in termination of access privileges to all company systems, as well as prompt surrender of organization-owned laptops, phones, and tablets. The email access of terminated employees who owned their own phones and tablets should be terminated immediately.

Ease of Use versus Security

Mavericks also assess the "ease of use" versus "security" tradeoffs. For example, authentication of users should include multi-factor authentication for important systems. Multifactor authentication creates another step of ID verification, an extra barrier between potential attackers and your data. Encryption is a process of protecting your sensitive business information by using a software program to make the information unreadable to anyone not having the encryption key. With encryption, even if a bad actor somehow obtains your data, it will be unusable without the keys to unencrypt the data. Multi-factor authentication and encryption of data are rapidly becoming must-haves, and can be deployed with a reasonable degree of ease of use compared to the elevated security provided.

The Equifax (and many other breaches) were caused by the failure to install patches to known compromises in software and systems. Software and hardware vendors regularly release patches and updates to their supported products to correct security problems and to improve functionality. Once a software patch is released, bad actors review the patch and accompanying information to identify the issue, and armed with this information, they can exploit the vulnerability. This vulnerability will exist inside your organization until you update the appropriate program with the patch. Mavericks ensure that their IT organizations understand how critical it is to apply the patches as soon as possible and employ a corporate standard for deploying patches to all systems in a timely manner. It is critically important that the organization utilize a trusted third party to verify that organization policies and procedures are actually followed. As Equifax demonstrates, a CEO cannot always rely on IT management to conform to policies and procedures. The CEO must have a competent and reliable third party test the organization's implementation of policy and procedure on a regular basis. Patch management testing is an excellent place to start.

A Bring Your Own Device ("BYOD") policy allows employees to use personal devices (phones, tablets, computers, etc.) to access corporate resources. It is intended to allow employees to use any device they choose to perform their work functions. Lenders need to think carefully about BYOD programs, and if they elect to allow such a program, they need to put in place appropriate policies and procedures to tackle these issues and minimize the risks. Organizations should provide guidance to users on how they can use their own devices to process corporate and personal data. The policy should also be clear to employees that they can only process corporate data for approved corporate purposes.

Another security policy to consider implementing is "least privilege". Least privilege is the security principle that dictates giving each user the least access to data possible while still allowing them to complete their job effectively. By implementing least privilege, an organization better protects the sensitive information of its customers, organization, and partners, by limiting the number of people who can access the information and the variety of channels through which data can leave the organization.

In the end, hackers will continue to escalate their attacks. Organizations have to escalate their security efforts.

CHAPTER SEVEN

Housing Families: 2020 & Beyond

A harsh truth facing the industry is that housing perhaps may never again mean what it meant for much of the twentieth century. By 2020, we may be facing a housing market in some parts of the United States where rising prices have driven out many homebuyers. Alternatives such as tiny homes, modular housing, and rentals may be the only viable options for many consumers, and it behooves the mortgage industry to explore how it will respond to these market adjustments.

Renters

While homebuyers have plateaued over the last 10 years, renters are following a steep rise and are now at levels we haven't seen in the states since the 1960s. Almost 37% of the U.S.'s heads of household rent their homes, as of 2016, according to the Pew Research Center. While buying still remains a better value than renting, rising costs, limited credit, and lack of a down payment keep many potential

— 185 —

homebuyers out of the market. The truth is there are just not enough low-cost, starter homes out there for consumers. And some areas of the United States have adopted policies that are anti-housing growth, either intentionally, or not. The impact of overly restrictive zoning, difficult land use development regulations, 'impact fees', anti-development litigation and other regulatory impositions have made affordable housing truly unavailable for large segments of the population.

In San Francisco, teachers, police officers, firefighters, and many professionals cannot afford to buy a home. According to Curbed SF[55], "a market report from Paragon Real Estate Group lays it all on the line: San Francisco median house sales price soars to $1,500,000 in May. Suffice to say, that's an all-time high...according to Paragon economist Patrick Carlisle, it's almost double the price from the same period just five years ago in 2012." That's about $1,000 per square foot, and out of reach for all but the wealthiest or those with very high incomes.

Inventory Pain

Of course, the main factor in rising housing costs stems from shortfalls in inventory. On the production side of housing, the question of inventory shortages relates directly to labor shortages in construction. Modular housing, perhaps built in tandem with robot labor in lieu of human labor, may be the way forward for an industry suffering from a dearth of housing solutions.

According to Prashant Gopal and Heather Perlberg writing at Bloomberg, modular constructions are not only becoming more

---

[55] https://sf.curbed.com/2017/6/7/15758460/median-home-price-sf

complex, but also more appealing. As the complexity of the modular home increases and as shipments of these manufactured structures continues to grow, these solutions are likely to become more appealing to a wider range of homebuyers.[56] It's not just millennials who are embracing manufactured housing over site-built properties. Many retirees are also turning to these lower cost homes as a viable solution for retirement.[57]

While all of this is promising, pursuing new forms of inventory (such as manufactured and modular housing) may require a cultural shift within the mortgage industry. There are several conversations we as an industry must have to drive this shift. The most crucial revolves around consumer choice when it comes to homebuying. Bigger is not always better. The consumer is beginning to understand this, but the mortgage industry sometimes digs its heels in against it.

On the obvious level, we are an industry in which salespeople are compensated on commissions based on the size of loans. Naturally, the inclination across the industry is to, then, sell higher balance loans. The subtler issue at play here is, however, that many in the industry don't even understand that manufactured housing is a viable product or a quality product.

Cody Pearce of Cascade spoke pretty passionately on this point during our conversation. He has seen a good deal of misunderstanding in the industry regarding manufactured housing as a solution for both inventory pain points and high home costs. "A lot of lenders don't know anyone who lives in manufactured housing... but it's a wonderful product. It's built to HUD code, and it meets all the

---

[56] https://www.census.gov/data/tables/time-series/econ/mhs/latest-data.html
[57] http://time.com/4710619/the-home-of-the-future/

requirements of other types of housing." Cody even had a learning curve with "MH" (Manufactured Housing) for some of his own team members at Cascade. What he has focused on is creating an ethos at the company that makes it clear that MH is a much-needed solution to a real problem. "We're serving the American Dream through affordable homeownership... I believe it is one of the key solutions to the affordable housing deficit that we have in the United States. I think manufactured housing is currently and will continue to play a significant role in filling the affordable housing void."

Of course, not all consumers are ready for this. Kevin Pearson observed that many consumers are just renting longer and entering the market at what would have been a second or third step, the "upgraded" home. "Our cycle has been interrupted," he observed citing the fact that few consumers understand that manufactured housing or other such options could serve as a first step before transitioning to an upgrade.

These options may soon be the *only* option for a large sector of homebuyers. As of April 2017, the average sale price of manufactured housing was $73,000.[58] In regions such as Washington D.C. or Silicon Valley, that type of affordable option for the average middle-class family is a pipe dream at the moment. The required annual income to afford the median house price in Northern Virginia, as an example, is $30,000 above the median income for the region. Offering a price point that is so much more manageable for the average consumer and with a product that has improved dramatically, why can't manufactured housing be an important piece of the puzzle? Modular home or prefab solutions have even become stylish for many consumers and attractive to builders looking for

---

[58] https://www.census.gov/data/tables/time-series/econ/mhs/latest-data.html

smaller, faster jobs in a slow market.[59] The mortgage industry needs to respond to this trend and consider it as a viable option in an ever-evolving marketplace.

The Environmental Impact on Housing in the Future

There can be no conversation around housing in the future without addressing the environmental impact on housing. One has to consider the natural disaster impact on housing arising from flooding in Texas and Florida and wildfires in California. One also has to consider the potential impact from seismic events and other natural disasters.

In the case of flooding, while the impact is localized for now to a few regions around the country, the impact felt in these regions is instantaneous and has dramatic results. As an example, home sales in New Orleans dropped by almost one quarter in the year following Hurricane Katrina. In the aftermath of Sandy, 39,000 people were still unhomed three years after the storm.[60] Much of this burden, of course, falls on lower income individuals already underserved by the mortgage industry. And regulation steps in once again to rear its ugly head—oftentimes, in the aftermath of large-scale natural disasters, the government has stepped in to impose regulations on future builds and rebuilds.

Locales such as Houston, for example, have properties that have flooded 4 or more times in the last 20 years. According to USA

---

[59] http://www.builderonline.com/building/10-things-you-need-to-know-about-modular-homes_o

[60] https://www.theatlantic.com/business/archive/2015/08/hurricane-katrina-sandy-disaster-recovery-/400244/

Today, "NFIP embraces a "flood-rebuild-repeat" model that has spawned an almost $25 billion debt. The National Wildlife Federation estimated in 1998 that 2% of properties covered by federal flood insurance had multiple damage claims accounting for 40% of flood insurance outlays, and that more than 5,000 homes had repeat claims exceeding their property value. A recent Pew Charitable Trust study revealed that 1% of the 5 million properties insured have produced almost a third of the damage claims and half the debt.

Preventing these types of recurring losses only makes sense. More robust building codes, too, are intended to protect the homeowner in the long run, but lead to higher fees on development, the cost of which extends to the consumer in the end. As hurricane seasons become more intense or the inevitable "Big One" takes place along the San Andreas Fault, the mortgage industry needs to consider the real-world impact of natural disasters on housing inventory and prices.

Technological Change

Tim Nguyen of BeSmartee sees a day when the time from application to close could be very short—limited only to the TRID mandated disclosure periods. Tim was one of the early interviews I did, and I thought Tim was overly optimistic. Not so much now. Tim (as well as the other 24 CEOs referenced herein) are Mavericks. They see the future, and how it can be meaningfully different.

Collectively, the 25 CEOs see the forces of change that will take closing a loan from 45 days to 10 or less. The 10 days could be much less if TRID were not involved. And eventually, consumer and industry pressure will remove some of the well intentioned but functionally difficult regulatory burdens.

One can imagine a blockchain-secured source of trusted historical and current data regarding a borrower. Collateral value on the home they intend to purchase could be obtained in a few minutes, with full approval including any conditions provided seconds thereafter. It seems surreal to a long-term industry participant. Yet we obtain a complete, up-to-date credit report in a few minutes. Why can't this happen with bank and income data? Fannie Mae can deliver some of that data currently with Day 1 Certainty, and Single Source promises a not-to-distant future where loan processing will not look anything like it does today.

Think about the possibilities of making a firm loan commitment, with all conditions, in seconds. Credit card providers deliver an unsecured credit decision today in just a few seconds. As my daughter pointedly mentioned, a *car dealer's F&I department* can shop multiple lenders and have a car buyer committed and closed in under an hour. The customer can drive the car away the same day.

Dave Stevens, the MBA and many lenders are right to worry about the Bright Line between primary origination and the secondary market GSEs. As mortgage bankers, there is a lot to ponder. Can blockchain, D1C, Single Source, Collateral Underwriter, instant online homeowners' insurance binders and other tools be arranged to provide a firm commitment with air-tight conditions? How does one compete with that? What if the servicers can use big data combined with tools to provide a refinance at will, without the customer even asking? "Hello Mr. Deitch, we noticed your 7/1 ARM resets in two years, but we can lower your rate by ½% and reset it for another seven years. Sign these documents and the deal is done." Not as far-fetched as I once thought.

While the mechanical manufacturing process can be significantly simplified, what about good advice? A trusted advisor will always have a valued place within a customer's heart and mind. Remember the fixed commissions in common stock trading? Trading 200 shares of IBM cost $400 thirty years ago with Merrill Lynch. It can now be done for less than $15 with most discount brokers. But for many, the need for trusted advice and perspective is valuable, and customers are willing to pay 50 to 100 basis points per year of investable assets to get it. The customer knows they could trade for a few dollars per hundred shares, but willingly pay much more for trusted advice. The commodity element of stock trading has been priced close to zero, but trusted advice is still priced at a premium. The advice is just paid for in an annual fee, as opposed to stock transactions.

So how will mortgage bankers adapt to the changing landscape? The value of "getting the loan done" will diminish, but the value of how to structure the transaction will open opportunities for trusted advice. The servicing asset may become the key to a customer for life. Technology could truly make closing a mortgage as fast and easy as getting a credit card, so 'owning' the customer relationship (servicing) may become a strategic imperative. How will banks and IMBs compete for these relationships?

Bill Cosgrove imagines a competitive landscape defined by the technology of predictive analytics to, in his words, "collect data and collect customers." With many LO's transitioning from face-to-face interactions to virtual customer relationships, he sees this type of technology as the most effective way for companies to find and engage prospects. Some will "swing and miss" he says, but there will also be a lot of home runs with this technological approach.

Disruption is everywhere. Cable TV cord cutters. Electric automobiles that can drive themselves. IPhones that double capability every two years. Airliners that can land without human intervention. Biologically customized drugs that fight cancer using the patient's genes to deliver the drug payload only to the cancer cells. Facial recognition. How do mortgage bankers adapt, prosper, and become effective disruptors?

New Blood in the Industry

One question I asked again and again to the CEOs I spoke with was "what would you say to the young person entering the mortgage industry today?" Answers varied, but consistent themes one would expect came up—work hard, focus on a niche, don't jump around, and so on.

Jerry Rader advised that those new to the industry start from a place of self-assessment. "Identify your core values." With this knowledge in hand, Jerry recommends, one can then head toward and develop one's own niche in the industry. Be confident, not arrogant, he encourages. A high-level goal at his company, in fact, has always been to develop leaders.

Jim MacLeod had a good deal of optimism for the "fresh perspective" those new to mortgage banking can bring. He sees new voices as not only bringing in a new vision, but also questioning how things are done and bringing a new enthusiasm for change and evolution.

Julie Piepho's advice was direct: "Learn, learn, learn, learn." Julie believes that there isn't anything a newbie to mortgage banking can learn that won't help him or her excel. She recommends network-ing widely, too, as a way to inform one's particular niche or subset and build connections. The best summary of her advice is essen-tially "be passionate", and it is advice that makes sense.

Bill Emerson encouraged us as an industry to do more to recruit out of college, showing young applicants that mortgage banking is a career one can choose instead of stumbling into. He sees a lot of opportunity for a voracious learner. He sees opportunity, in fact, ahead for the industry as a whole: "I think there's a massive amount of opportunity... it's just a matter of whether we look at it as oppor-tunity or we look at it as challenges." It's this kind of clear vision and ability to change perspective, perhaps, that makes the maverick CEO excel. Some interesting answers came when the conversation segued into what could be envisioned for the industry as a whole moving forward. It became clear through these conversations that the way through for the mortgage industry will require adjustments to changing demographics, for one.

Susan Stewart was particularly clear-headed and blunt on this point: "We just need to have more diversification than we have today because that's the world." She is optimistic, however, about the industry making this adjustment, provided it takes an "inside out" approach and addresses some of the negative patterns of the last several years. "I think the lending community will find a way to create what is necessary, but it's going to have to get driven from within the lending community ... we were going down that road 10 years ago... we just got off the path... Bad behavior took over and it became not about creating a product for our chang-ing demography—it became about creating a product that had a better yield." Ultimately, she says, the pragmatic answer is to hire employees from the communities we as an industry will be targeting to inform the process and develop products that resonate effectively. Stan Middleman's clear-headed advice to new recruits perhaps applies to the industry as a whole and is worth considering: "Learn to learn."

The Path Forward

No author of a book can resist providing their personal view of the Path Forward. The mortgage industry is in for a period of adjustment over the next several years. Outstanding customer satisfaction and superior profitability will be the metrics of success. "Human Spackle" and FinTech Band-Aids won't work long term.

For individual lenders, the thought leadership of the mavericks provides guidance on the mortgage value chain:

Generally, much reduction in revenue leakage and much improvement in customer satisfaction can arise from transformation of a lender's process, workflow and technology in the context of the lender's vision, culture, served markets, desired customer experience and desired service and profitability levels. This is not a difficult process, but it is time consuming and takes a concerted effort across the lender's value chain. Note that this process is not 'best practice' – rather it is choosing the *right processes, workflow and technology* to deliver the lender's desired customer experience to the selected served markets. These served markets include geography, loan product, channel, and delivery methods.

Sometimes the entire process is difficult to tackle at once. The best approach is the end-to-end review, starting at the back of the process and working forward. Following are a few ideas to get started if you're not quite ready to tackle the whole end-to-end process:

Disrupt yourself: Evaluate existing business models much as a hacker would try and beat your security safeguards. Identify the business model vulnerabilities. Summarizing Tim Nguyen of BeSmartee: Identify the weak points of your lending model that are hard to see. In mortgage banking, one weakness is the process of collecting data from borrowers. Adapt and innovate in a way that you can disrupt yourself.

Build on initial successes: Establish a culture of "Try It. Fix It. Try It Again." Encourage testing and piloting new technologies, not necessarily passing and failing them. A specific problem that a technology could solve is a great candidate for "Try It. Fix It. Try It Again." This harks back to the initial tech revolution at the turn of the 19th century. Thomas Edison innovated by trying a lot, failing a lot, but finding transformative technologies in the process.

Try a Tech-Scrum: Form a team to get dirty with some emerging tech and see what problems can be quickly solved in an innovative way. As Maylin Casanueva, a colleague, often says, "Don't wait for a checklist or plan. Just try it." Nima Ghamsari of Blend related that small steps taken frequently result in big gains.

Tackle Resistance Head On: Al Stanley, CIO of Angel Oak Capital recently said, "I don't stay in my swim lane. Some CIOs are 'Chief Interference Officers'. We need

Chief Innovation Officers in lender IT organizations." Push boundaries and expect resistance, especially from legacy IT resources. Legacy IT can be an enabler or an inhibitor. The key is knowing how to turn existing infrastructure into a competitive advantage.

Be Open Minded: Don't focus on a specific technology. Envision how your company's ecosystem can be different tomorrow than today. Build capability to leverage existing assets. There are excellent adjunct solutions that can leverage an existing technology.

Build Alliances: For example, the existing US Air Traffic Control ("ATC") System still has vacuum tube powered vestiges and still uses paper slips to track aircraft in some control towers. The ATC system used alliances to leverage the legacy system with airborne technology powered aircraft collision avoidance, software enabled aircraft runway conflict alerts and to deliver ATC data to anyone seeking real time airline status via FlightAware.Com. If the government can do it, why can't you?

The lenders that are first to effectively complete this transformation will likely achieve superior customer satisfaction, superior profitability, high quality loan packages, and high levels of employee retention. Transformation is not optional; the only question is *how quickly* a lender chooses to undertake it. And transformation is not an add-on activity. It requires a commitment of time and resources from the CEO to the front line. Freshly envisioning the business from the *back end of the process and moving forward* to Initial Customer Interest is essential.

At the industry level, executives, legislators, and regulators need to come together to discuss how to move forward and jointly tackle the challenges of regulatory cost, lack of product innovation, the material number of underserved borrowers, the level of profit and the tendency for high profit volatility, the application of transformational technology, and the affordability of housing discussed in this book.

Finally, the privilege of holding one-on-one conversations with industry thought leaders invariably generated insights for both parties. Consider more active participation in industry conferences, peer groups, and engagement.

My next step: additional invitations to C-level executives to engage in one-on-one discussions regarding key topics within this book. And I'd very much welcome your outreach to me to initiate that engagement.

My very best to the reader,

Jim Deitch, January 2018

APPENDIX 1
The Mavericks

Barrett Burns

M r. Burns serves as the President and Chief Executive Officer of VantageScore Solutions, LLC. Over the years of serving in the industry, he developed extensive experience in banking and finance that allowed him to hold executive positions in a variety of companies. He serves as a board member for numerous industry associations including the Mortgage Bankers Association, the Structured Finance Industry Group Executive Committee, America's Homeowner Alliance, the Corporate Board of Governors for the National Association of Hispanic Real Estate Professionals, and the Asian Real Estate Association of America's National Advisory Council.

Bill Cosgrove

Mr. Cosgrove began his mortgage banking career in 1986 as a residential loan officer. In 1994, he joined Union Home Mortgage Corp. and four years later became the President. Later, he earned the Mortgage

Bankers Association's Certified Mortgage Banker certificate. Throughout his career, Mr. Cosgrove has demonstrated strong leadership that led to successful outcomes. In 2007-2008, Mr. Cosgrove was President of the Ohio Mortgage Bankers Association. In 2008 & 2013, he earned the coveted Hodupp Award for his many contributions to the Ohio MBA. From 2008 to 2010, Bill was the National Chairman for MBA's MORPAC Committee.

Bill Emerson

Mr. Emerson serves as the Vice Chairman of Rock Holdings Inc., the parent company of Quicken Loans, the nation's second largest mortgage lender. Bill joined Quicken loans in 1993 and served with passion and commitment to helping customers. The strong leadership skills led Quicken Loans to become the largest retail mortgage lender and has closed nearly $300 Billion in home loan volume across all 50 states since 2013. Bill is a member of the Board of Directors of Xenith, Inc., the Detroit Economic Club, and The Parade Company and the Skillman Foundation.

Byron Boston

Since January 1, 2014 Mr. Byron L. Boston has been the Chief Executive Officer and Co-Chief Investment Officer of Dynex Capital, Inc. In addition to his current role, Byron has also been the President and Executive Vice President of Dynex Capital. Before Dynex Capital, he served as a Vice Chairman, Chief Investment Officer and Executive Vice President of Sunset Financial Resources Inc. He has also served as Vice President and Co-Manager of The Mortgage Portfolio Group of Federal Home Loan Mortgage Corporation (Freddie Mac).

Cody Pearce

Mr. Pearce is the President and Co-founder of Cascade Financial Services, LLC. He is known for his efforts in improving the company's growth and culture. Mr. Pearce currently serves as Vice Chairman of MHI's Financial Services Division, Board member of MHI, is the former Chairman of the MBA's State Legislative and Regulatory Committee, serves on both MORPAC and MHIPac Committees and is the Former Chairman of the MHI of AZ. Most recently Mr. Pearce was appointed by the Governor of Arizona to sit on the Arizona Board of Manufactured Housing.

David Motley

Mr. Motley, a Certified Mortgage Banker, has been working with Colonial Savings for more than 15 years. He has been the Executive Vice President and moved his way up to serve as the President of Banking and Mortgage Operations at Colonial Savings, F.A. in May 2006. David Motley has more than 25 years of mortgage production management experience. Motley serves on the board of the Texas Mortgage Bankers Association as the Secretary/ Treasurer.

Dave Stevens

Since June 2011, Mr. Stevens has been serving as the Chief Executive Officer and President of the Mortgage Bankers Association (MBA). He has a well-rounded background from working with Long & Foster Real Estate, Inc. in the role of Senior Vice President then as the President and Chief Operating Officer. In addition, he served as the Senior Vice President of Mortgage Sourcing and Single-Family

Lending at Freddie Mac. He sits on the Board of Directors for the National Association of Mortgage Brokers (NAMB) and on the lenders advisory council for the Mortgage Bankers Association (MBA). He was the Founding Executive Sponsor of the Woman's Mortgage Industry Network and coordinated the first Latino initiative joint venture with Freddie Mac and Latino mortgage industry leaders.

Debra Still

Ms. Still is the Chief Executive Officer and President of Pulte Mortgage LLC. She has been serving the mortgage industry for more than three decades. Her background has allowed her to take many roles in Pulte Mortgage LLC. She was an Executive Vice President of Loan Production; member of the Board of Directors; Corporate Secretary, and Chief Operating Officer. Ms. Still served as Chairman of the Residential Board of Governors at Mortgage Bankers Association.

Ed Robinson

Mr. Edward Robinson has been leading Fifth Third Mortgage since July 2016. Prior to this role, he served as a Senior Vice President of Lending Servicing Operations and Vice President of Origination. In addition, he has held positions in Genworth Financial and General Electric, where he was responsible for directing operations for the U.S. Mortgage Insurance business, leading strategic initiatives for long-term care insurance, and financial management and analytics.

Jamie Korus-Pearce

Ms. Jamie Korus-Pearce started her career as a loan originator in 2002. She quickly moved into the position as the President and Principal at Alliance Financial Resources, LLC in 2006. Jamie currently serves on the Board of Directors, Residential Board of Governors, and the Advisory Board of the MBA Opens Doors Foundation.

Jerry Rader

Mr. Rader has the current role as the President of Corridor Mortgage Group. Throughout his career he has focused on personal integrity and customer satisfaction. These two factors have led Corridor Mortgage Group to be the leading lender in the East Coast since 2000. Before his position at Corridor Mortgage Group, he was a Loan Officer, Branch Manager, and Vice President of Capital Mortgage Finance.

Jerry Schiano

Mr. Schiano has more than 20 years of mortgage lending experience in sales and a variety of executive management positions. His expertise led him to form New Penn Financial in March 2008. Today Jerry, serves as the President and Chief Executive Officer of New Penn Financial. He also serves as a Director of Shellpoint Partners, LLC.

James MacLeod

Mr. MacLeod, also known as Jim, serves as the Executive Chairman of CoastalSouth Bancshares, Inc. and CoastalStates Bank. Previously, he was Chief Operating Officer, Senior Managing Director and Chief Executive Officer of the Homeowners Mortgage Enterprise, Inc. He is a Member of both the Mortgage Bankers Association of America and the Mortgage Bankers Association of the Carolinas.

Jonathan Corr

Mr. Corr serves as the Chief Executive Officer and President of Ellie Mae, Inc. Before he became CEO and President, Jonathan focused on marketing, strategy, and product management. He is recognized for his expertise and has served in marketing and product management positions for Apple Computer, Tandem, Compaq, and Netscape. He has also served as the Chief Strategy Officer and Executive Vice President of Business Development and Product Strategy for Ellie Mae, Inc.

Julie Piepho

Ms. Piepho is President-National Operations – Cornerstone Home Lending, Inc. She joined the mortgage industry in 1977. In her career, she has led teams of sales and operation to a successful outcome, through her strategic planning and handling organizational changes. In 2013, Julie was awarded the E. Michael Rosser Lifetime Achievement Award, which is given to individuals that show the highest principles, ethics, and professional values of the Colorado

Mortgage Lenders Association. Outside of work, Julie has a passion for helping people and dedicates her time to the Alzheimer's Association and Habitat for Humanity.

Kevin Pearson

Mr. Pearson serves as President of CalAtlantic Financial Services (formerly RMC Mortgage and Standard Pacific Mortgage), CalAtlantic Title (formerly Ryland Title Company and Standard Pacific Title) and CalAtlantic Insurance Services (formerly Ryland Insurance Services), a collective group of legal entities wholly owned by CalAtlantic Group (formerly Standard Pacific, Corp. and The Ryland Group, Inc.). He previously served as an executive in Bank of America's Builder Joint Venture group, and a Senior Vice President of GMAC.

Martin Kerr

Mr. Kerr is the President of Bestborn Business Solutions, the company behind Loan Vision. Martin has experience in this industry and has a focus in creating efficiencies in the workflow process of the mortgage industry. Before his position at Bestborn, he was a project and business system manager for Technical Plastics.

Nathan Burch

Mr. Burch is currently the Chief Executive Officer and Principal of Vellum Mortgage. Through the efforts of leadership, he has made a positive impact in the positions he's held in his career. Nathan is the founder of McLean Mortgage Corporation, a company that was recognized in 2013 as the "47th Largest Mortgage Lender" by Scotsman Guide and the "10 Best Mortgage Company to Work For" by Mortgage Executive Magazine.

Nima Ghamsari

Mr. Ghamsari serves as Chief Executive and Co-founder of Blend, a Silicon Valley Technology company empowering lenders to originate efficiently while keeping a user friendly interface. Prior to his position at Blend, Nima was a business development engineer and worked as an advisor for the CEO of Palantir Technologies.

Patty Arvielo

Ms. Arvielo is the President & Co-founder of New American Funding. She is a natural leader and has a strong commitment to helping individuals in her industry and community. Patricia is deeply involved with the National Association of Hispanic Real Estate Professionals, an organization that is increasing the rate of sustainable Hispanic homeownership. Throughout her career she was recognized for her efforts and received the National Hispanic Business Women Association in 2014 and the NHBWA Business Woman of the year.

Patrick Sinks

Mr. has been the Chief Executive Officer and Director of MGIC Investment Corp. He has held many positions within MGIC's finance and accounting organizations, where he was positioned as Senior Vice President, Controller and Chief Accounting Officer.

Phil DeFronzo

Mr. DeFronzo is the founder and CEO of Norcom Mortgage, through natural leadership Phil was able to grow the company to a well-known Regional Lender. His achievements include increasing revenue, building brand awareness, and growing the business. In 2011, Norcom was recognized as one of the "Fastest Growing Lenders in New England."

Rich Bennion

Mr. Bennion serves as the Executive Vice President at HomeStreet, Inc. Before this position Rich was the Executive Vice President and Director of Residential Construction and Affiliated Businesses, and Single-Family Lending Director. Since 2004, Rich has been a Member of the Fannie Mae Western Business Center Advisory Board.

Stanley Middleman

Mr. Middlemen founded Freedom Mortgage Corporation in 1990 and currently serves as the Chairman and Chief Executive Officer. In addition, he has been a Non-Executive Chairman of Cherry Hill Mortgage Investment Corporation since 2012 and a member of the MBA. Stan has more than 27 years of experience in financial and residential mortgage markets.

Steve Shank

Mr. Shank serves as Chief Executive Officer and President, Operations of Flinchbaugh Engineering, Inc. (FEI). Mr. Shank joined FEI in 2005 with 15 years' experience in an engineered-to-order manufacturing environment. He served in leadership roles in various functional areas, including customer service, accounting and operations. He has broad experience in the implementation of Lean practices and the use of Six Sigma tools. Mr. Shank has a Bachelor of Science Degree in Finance from the University of Delaware.

Susan Stewart

Ms. Stewart is the President and CEO of SWBC Mortgage Corporation. Susan has impacted her company tremendously, she is well known for her commitment amongst her customers and co-workers. She serves as Vice Chair of the Residential Board of Governors of the MBA, as well as MBA's Opens Doors Foundation.

Tim Nguyen

Mr. Nguyen is the Co-founder and CEO of BeSmartee, which is the leader in digital mortgage innovation. Using a combination of big data and artificial intelligence, borrowers can go from application to approval to disclosures, and enter underwriting in about 15 minutes. He was also a Co-founder and Chief Executive Officer of InHouse, Inc. a technology-enabled-service company providing appraisal management solutions to the mortgage lending industry.

APPENDIX 2

The Financial Crisis of 2007-2010 and Beyond

The extreme stress in the financial markets in the late summer and early fall of 2008 was quantified by the Kansas City Financial Stress Index (KCFSI), a monthly measure of stress in the U.S. financial system based on 11 financial market variables issued by the Kansas City Federal Reserve Bank. A positive value indicates that financial stress is above the long-run average, while a negative value signifies that financial stress is below the long-run average. The KCFSI decreased from 1.47 in April 2008 to 0.94 in May 31, 2008 . . . followed by an almost six-fold increase to an all-time high of 5.55 as of October 2008. This unexpected and unprecedented increase in financial stress as quantified by the KCFSI was the proximate cause of rapid declines in asset prices.

KANSAS CITY FRB FINANCIAL STRESS INDEX 2008-2009

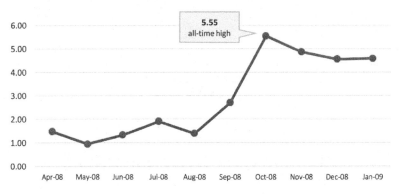

Source: The Federal Reserve Bank of Kansas City

The failure of several subprime mortgage lenders in 2007 reduced the availability of credit to subprime borrowers. New Century Financial Corporation, a real estate investment trust founded in 1995 and headquartered in Irvine, California declared bankruptcy on April 2, 2007. On July 11, 2007, credit rating agencies S&P and Moody's announced the downgrade of $12 billion and $5 billion of subprime RMBS, respectively. Bear Stearns placed two structured and asset-backed securities hedge funds in bankruptcy on July 31, 2007. American Home Mortgage Investment Corp., a large subprime lender, filed for bankruptcy on August 6, 2007. In 2007, losses on subprime mortgage-related financial assets began to cause strains in the global financial markets. In December 2007, the U.S. economy entered a recession.

Despite the failures cited above, the markets in early 2008 did not act as if the economy was in severe trouble. On January 11, 2008, for example, Bank of America announced an agreement to purchase Countrywide Financial Corp for $4 billion in stock. Bear Stearns was acquired by JPMorgan Chase on March 16, 2008. The Federal

Reserve agreed to guarantee $30 billion of Bear Stearns' assets in connection with the government-sponsored sale of the investment bank to JPMorgan Chase.

As of late May 2008, the financial markets continued to show signs of stress, but the stress was largely confined to the subprime market, and significant actions by the Federal Reserve and other central banks appeared to be addressing subprime mortgage matters. For example, the Federal Reserve responded to an apparent lack of liquidity in worldwide financial markets with sharp reductions in the federal funds rate, reducing the rate from 5.25% in May 2007 to 2.00% as of April 30, 2008. The Federal Reserve press release stated, "The substantial easing of monetary policy to date, combined with ongoing measures to foster market liquidity, should help to promote moderate growth over time and to mitigate risks to economic activity." On May 8, 2008, the Federal Reserve provided an increase in the amounts auctioned to eligible depository institutions under its biweekly Term Auction Facility ("TAF") to bring the amounts outstanding under the TAF to $150 billion, again to increase liquidity.

For example, prior to the failure of Fannie Mae, the company issued the following unexpected and extraordinary description of events occurring after the close of its second quarter 2008 (the note below was included in Fannie Mae's June 30, 2008, Form 10-Q, released August 9, 2008):

Market Events of July 2008:

> *In mid-July, following the close of the second quarter, liquidity and trading levels in the capital markets became extremely volatile, and the functioning of the markets was*

disrupted. The market value of our common stock dropped rapidly, to its lowest level since October 1990, and we experienced reduced demand for our unsecured debt and MBS products. This market disruption caused a significant increase in our cost of funding and a substantial increase in mark-to-market losses on our trading securities arising from a significant widening of credit spreads. In addition, during July, credit performance continued to deteriorate, and we recorded charge-offs and foreclosed property expenses that were higher than we had experienced in any month during the second quarter and higher than we expected, driven by higher defaults and higher loan loss severities in markets most affected by the steep home price declines. Greater credit losses in July not only reduce our July net income through our actual realized losses, but also affect us as we expect that we will need to make further increases to our combined loss reserves in the second half of 2008 to incorporate our experience in July.

Less than 30 days after this 10-Q release, in early September 2008, Fannie Mae was in unexpected conservatorship. In addition, four other major publicly traded companies were unexpectedly placed in conservatorship, bankruptcy or acquired under duress. The companies and their impact on the financial services marketplace listed below in September 2008 were extraordinary:

- Freddie Mac and Fannie Mae owned or guaranteed $4 trillion in mortgage loans at the time of their failure, or 40% of all residential mortgage loans outstanding in the U.S.

- AIG had assets of over $1 trillion at the time of its takeover.

- Washington Mutual and Wachovia assets totaled over $1 trillion at the time of their takeover.

The failure of these five financial firms, with a collective total of $6 trillion of assets heavily involved in the U.S. housing market, in one month (September 6 to October 7, 2008), had an overwhelming adverse impact on liquidity and price discovery in financial markets.

The unexpected nature of the stress in the financial markets is illustrated in the sharp climb in bank failures. Total assets of failed banks from the beginning of 2007 through June 1, 2008 were just under $5 billion. By October 1, 2008 the total assets of failed banks had grown to $350 billion, an increase of 70 times. A total of 7 banks failed from January 1, 2005 to June 4, 2008. Another 27 failed from June 1, 2008 to January 31, 2009. Ultimately, 468 banks with total assets of $690 billion failed from January 1, 2005 through December 31, 2012.

On July 11, 2008, IndyMac Bank, F.S.B., Pasadena, CA, was closed by the Office of Thrift Supervision. The Federal Deposit Insurance Corporation was named conservator. IndyMac Bank, FSB had total assets of $32.01 billion and total deposits of $19.06 billion as of March 31, 2008. The prior FDIC-insured failure in California was the Southern Pacific Bank, Torrance, on February 7, 2003.

On July 13, 2008, the Board of Governors of the Federal Reserve System announced that it had granted the Federal Reserve Bank of New York the authority to lend to Fannie Mae and Freddie Mac should such lending prove necessary and that any lending would be at the primary credit rate and collateralized by U.S. government and federal agency securities. This authorization was intended to supplement the Treasury's existing lending authority and to help ensure the ability of Fannie Mae and Freddie Mac to promote the availability of home mortgage credit during a period of stress in financial markets. At the same time, the U.S. Treasury Department announced a temporary increase in the credit lines of Fannie Mae and Freddie Mac and a temporary authorization for the Treasury to purchase equity in either GSE if needed.

On July 15, 2008, the Securities and Exchange Commission issued an emergency order to enhance investor protections against "naked" short selling in the securities of Fannie Mae, Freddie Mac, and primary dealers at commercial and investment banks.

On July 30, 2008, President Bush signed the Housing and Economic Recovery Act of 2008 (Public Law 110-289), which, among other provisions, authorized the Treasury to purchase GSE obligations and reforms the regulatory supervision of the GSEs under a new Federal Housing Finance Agency.

On July 30, 2008, the Federal Reserve announced several steps to enhance the effectiveness of its existing liquidity facilities, including the introduction of longer terms to maturity in its Term Auction Facility Extension of the Primary Dealer Credit Facility (PDCF) and the Term Securities Lending Facility (TSLF).

The Federal Housing Finance Agency (FHFA) initiated the conservatorships of the Federal National Mortgage Association (Fannie Mae) and the Federal Home Loan Mortgage Corporation (Freddie Mac) on September 6, 2008. The U.S. Treasury Department announced three additional measures to complement the FHFA's decision: 1) Preferred stock purchase agreements between the Treasury/FHFA and Fannie Mae and Freddie Mac to ensure the GSEs positive net worth; 2) a new secured lending facility available to

Fannie Mae, Freddie Mac, and the Federal Home Loan Banks; and 3) a temporary program to purchase GSE MBS.

On September 14, 2008, the Federal Reserve Board announced a significant broadening in the collateral accepted under its existing liquidity program for primary dealers and financial markets to provide additional support to financial markets.

On September 15, 2008, Bank of America announced its intent to purchase Merrill Lynch & Co. for $50 billion.

Also, on September 15, 2008 Lehman Brothers filed for federal bankruptcy protection.

Credit rating agencies downgraded AIG's long-term credit rating on the afternoon of September 15, 2008. AIG's stock price plunged. AIG could not access short-term liquid funds in the credit markets.

On September 16, 2008, the Federal Reserve Board, with the full support of the Treasury Department, authorized the Federal Reserve Bank of New York to lend up to $85 billion to AIG under section 13(3) of the Federal Reserve Act.

The net asset value of shares in the Reserve Primary Money Fund fell below $1, primarily due to losses on Lehman Brothers commercial paper and medium-term notes, further disrupting liquidity in the money markets.

On September 17, 2008, the Securities and Exchange Commission took several coordinated actions to strengthen investor protections against "naked" short selling. The Commission's actions applied to the securities of all public companies, including all companies in the financial sector. The actions were effective at 12:01 a.m. ET on Thursday, September 18, 2008.

On September 18, 2008, the Bank of Canada, the Bank of England, the European Central Bank (ECB), the Federal Reserve, the Bank of Japan, and the Swiss National Bank announced coordinated measures designed to address the continued elevated pressures in U.S. dollar short-term funding markets and to improve the liquidity conditions in global financial markets.

On September 19, 2008, the Federal Reserve Board announced two enhancements to its programs to provide liquidity to markets. One initiative extended non-recourse loans at the primary credit rate to U.S. depository institutions and bank holding companies to finance their purchases of high-quality asset-backed commercial paper (ABCP) from money market mutual funds. To further support market functioning, the Federal Reserve agreed to purchase from primary dealers quantities of federal agency discount notes, which are short-term debt obligations issued by Fannie Mae, Freddie Mac, and the Federal Home Loan Banks.

On September 19, 2008, the U.S. Treasury Department established a temporary guarantee program for the U.S. money market mutual fund industry. Concerns about the net asset value of money market funds falling below $1 exacerbated global financial market turmoil and caused severe liquidity strains in world markets. In turn, these pressures caused a spike in some short-term interest and funding rates, and significantly heightened volatility in exchange markets. Maintenance of the standard $1 net asset value for money market mutual funds was important to investors. If the net asset value for a fund fell below $1, this undermined investor confidence. The program provided support to investors in funds that participate in the program and those funds will not "break the buck". This action was to enhance market confidence and alleviate investors' concerns about the ability for money market mutual funds to absorb a loss.

The Exchange Stabilization Fund was established by the Gold Reserve Act of 1934. This Act authorizes the Secretary of the Treasury, with the approval of the President, "to deal in gold, foreign exchange, and other instruments of credit and securities" consistent with the obligations of the U.S. government in the International Monetary Fund to promote international financial stability.

On September 20, 2008, the Treasury Department submitted legislation to the Congress requesting authority to purchase troubled assets from financial institutions to promote market stability and help protect American families and the US economy.

On September 25, 2008, JPMorgan Chase acquired the banking operations of Washington Mutual Bank in a transaction facilitated by the Federal Deposit Insurance Corporation. JPMorgan Chase acquired the assets, assumed the qualified financial contracts and made a payment of $1.9 billion. Claims by equity, subordinated and senior debt holders were not acquired. Washington Mutual Bank also had a subsidiary, Washington Mutual FSB, Park City, Utah. They had combined assets of $307 billion and total deposits of $188 billion.

On September 29, 2008, central banks announced further coordinated actions to expand significantly the capacity to provide U.S. dollar liquidity. The Federal Reserve announced several initiatives to support financial stability and to maintain a stable flow of credit to the economy during this period of significant strain in global markets. Actions by the Federal Reserve included: (1) an increase in the size of the 84-day maturity TAF auctions to $75 billion per auction from $25 billion beginning with the October 6 auction, (2) two forward TAF auctions totaling $150 billion to be conducted in November to provide term funding over year-end, and (3) an increase in swap authorization limits with the Bank of Canada, Bank of England, Bank of Japan, Danmarks Nationalbank (National Bank of Denmark), European Central Bank (ECB), Norges Bank (Bank of Norway), Reserve Bank of Australia, Sveriges Riksbank (Bank of Sweden), and Swiss National Bank to a total of $620 billion, from $290 billion previously.

On September 29, 2008, Citigroup Inc. announced its intent to acquire the banking operations of Wachovia Corporation; Charlotte, North Carolina, in a transaction facilitated by the Federal Deposit Insurance Corporation and concurred with by the Board of Governors of the Federal Reserve and the Secretary of the Treasury in consultation with the President. (Wells Fargo & Company offered a competing bid on October 3, 2008, which ultimately was accepted.)

The Troubled Asset Relief Program ("TARP") was signed into law by U.S. President George W. Bush on October 3, 2008. TARP provided up to $700 billion to inject equity into the U.S. banks and to purchase 'troubled assets'.

On October 3, 2008, President George W. Bush signed the Emergency Economic Stabilization Act of 2008, which temporarily raised the basic limit on federal deposit insurance coverage from $100,000 to $250,000 per depositor. The temporary increase in deposit insurance coverage became effective upon the President's signature. The legislation provided that the basic deposit insurance limit would return to $100,000 after December 31, 2009. (In fact, the 'temporary' limit has remained at $250,000.)

On October 7, 2008, the Federal Reserve Board announced the creation of the Commercial Paper Funding Facility ("CPFF"), a facility that would complement the Federal Reserve's existing credit facilities to help provide liquidity to term funding markets.

On October 14, 2008, the Treasury announced a voluntary Capital Purchase Program to encourage U.S. financial institutions to build capital to increase the flow of financing to U.S. businesses and consumers and to support the U.S. economy. Under the program, Treasury purchased up to $250 billion of senior preferred shares on standardized terms as described in the program's term sheet. The senior preferred shares would qualify as Tier 1 capital.

On October 24, 2008, PNC Financial Services Group Inc. purchased National City Corporation, creating the fifth largest U.S. bank.

On November 10, 2008, the Federal Reserve Board and the U.S. Treasury Department announced a restructuring of the government's financial support of AIG. The Treasury was to purchase $40 billion of AIG preferred shares under the TARP program, a portion of which was to be used to reduce the Federal Reserve's loan to AIG from $85 billion to $60 billion. The Federal Reserve Board also authorized the Federal Reserve Bank of New York to establish two new lending facilities for AIG: The Residential Mortgage-Backed Securities Facility was to lend up to $22.5 billion to a newly formed limited liability company to purchase residential MBS from AIG; the Collateralized Debt Obligations Facility was to lend up to $30 billion to a newly formed LLC to purchase CDOs from AIG (Maiden Lane III LLC).

On November 18, 2008, Executives of Ford, General Motors, and Chrysler testified before Congress, requesting access to the TARP for federal loans.

On November 20, 2008, Fannie Mae and Freddie Mac announced that they would suspend mortgage foreclosures until January 2009.

On November 21, 2008, the U.S. Treasury Department announced that it would help liquidate The Reserve Fund's U.S. Government Fund. The Treasury served as a buyer of last resort for the fund's securities to ensure the orderly liquidation of the fund.

On November 21, 2008, the U.S. Treasury Department, Federal Reserve Board, and FDIC jointly announced an agreement with Citigroup that provided a package of guarantees, liquidity access, and capital. Citigroup issued preferred shares to the Treasury and FDIC in exchange for protection against losses on a $306 billion pool of commercial and residential securities held by Citigroup. The Federal Reserve was to backstop residual risk in the asset pool through a non-recourse loan. In addition, the Treasury committed up to an additional $20 billion in Citigroup from the TARP.

On November 25, 2008, the Federal Reserve Board announced the creation of the Term Asset-Backed Securities Lending Facility ("TALF"), under which the Federal Reserve Bank of New York would lend up to $200 billion on a non-recourse basis to holders of AAA-rated asset-backed securities and recently originated consumer and small business loans. The U.S. Treasury would provide $20 billion of TARP money for credit protection.

On November 25, 2008, the Federal Reserve Board announced a new program to purchase direct obligations of housing related government-sponsored enterprises —Fannie Mae, Freddie Mac and Federal Home Loan Banks—and MBS backed by the GSEs. Purchases of up to $100 billion in GSE direct obligations were to be conducted as auctions among Federal Reserve primary dealers.

Purchases of up to $500 billion in MBS were to be conducted by asset managers.

On December 3, 2008, the SEC approved measures to increase transparency and accountability at credit rating agencies to ensure that firms provide more meaningful ratings and greater disclosure to investors.

On December 19, 2008, the U.S. Treasury Department authorized loans of up to $13.4 billion for General Motors and $4.0 billion for Chrysler from the TARP.

On December 29, 2008, the U.S. Treasury Department announced that it would purchase $5 billion in equity from GMAC as part of its program to assist the domestic automotive industry. The Treasury also agreed to lend up to $1 billion to General Motors "so that GM can participate in a rights offering at GMAC in support of GMAC's reorganization as a bank holding company." This commitment was in addition to the support announced on December 19, 2008.

By any view, it was a hell of a six-month period.

The Book in Summary – For those who want the book in 10 minutes or less

T his Executive Summary distills the insights of 25 mavericks into about 20 pages. These transformative executives are mavericks not in the sense of the Tom Cruise character in Top Gun, but rather in the sense that they are groundbreakers. They embody and act on thought leadership that can create a high customer satisfaction, high profit, low cost, high employee retention business model for mortgage lending. Note that throughout this book, the term "high profit" means 100 basis points or more in pretax profit on loan origination activities.

How does a transformational executive create a high customer satisfaction, high profit, low cost, high employee retention business model? From speaking with 25 or so maverick CEOs, I have begun to understand it as a flowchart that starts with vision and ends with profitable financial results. Vision shapes culture which, in turn, shapes the desired customer experience, which then shapes process and workflow, which shapes technology choices, which then delivers profitable financial results.

Let's summarize each item:

Vision and Culture

How does the lender want to be viewed by the customer? How will the customer be treated? What can the customer expect from you? How does one convey that vision to potential customers, employees, third parties? Mavericks call this "Vision"[61], and from this vision comes culture. A few examples of Vision: New American Funding: "Your Mortgage, Your Terms." Freedom Mortgage: "Mortgage is our Specialty. Freedom to Dream the American Dream Your Way." Quicken Loans gives us "Mortgage Confidently". Fifth Third Mortgage: "Open the Door to Your Dream Home". Cascade Financial: "Serving the American Dream through Home Ownership". Corridor Mortgage: "Opening Doors to Your Future". HomeStreet Bank: "Your HomeStreet Loan". And a few non-lenders: Amazon: "Focused on the Customer". Southwest Airlines: "Customer Service delivered with a sense of warmth, friendliness, individual pride, and Company Spirit". These statements define vision as we will discuss it in this book and, in turn, foments a work culture that foments that Vision.

---

[61] This definition of 'vision' may not be the traditional business school definition, but this is how 'vision' is used herein.

At its core, the vision should communicate what your customer can expect. To this point, if the vision is not part of the fabric of your company's culture and public face, you are missing an opportunity to communicate it clearly and set the table for your customers' expectations of their experience.

You also need to consider every link in the chain, and the personal investment of everyone involved. As Jerry Rader put it in my discussion with him for this book, "People matter." He went on to elaborate that anyone—be they a customer, an employee, or a referral partner—has a story. "Every one of them has hopes and dreams, every one of them has a family." One must respect and honor their stories. This is a recurring theme with the Mavericks.

You'd be surprised how many lenders do not communicate their Vision (and the Culture that defines how employees deliver that Vision) to set the customer's expectations of the upcoming customer experience. If you get nothing else from this book, go straight to your website, marketing materials, employee manual, whatever else your customers and employees might be exposed to. How well are your company's Vision and Culture communicated? One company that exemplifies a cohesive culture that clearly communicates vision takes its vision to virtually everything.

Part of my research for this book took me to Southwest Airlines National Training Center in Dallas, TX. While visiting the facility for two days, I noted that Southwest Culture—Warrior Spirit, Servant's Heart, and 'FunLUVing' Attitude—was evident just about everywhere. Meeting rooms, engine repair training shops, and even the 'dunk tank' simulator for water evacuation training had examples of Southwest Culture's themes writ large. I even read about Southwest's "Warrior Experience" while using the urinal in

Southwest's new training facility in Dallas. The Southwest Culture was literally everywhere, including the tri-color 'heart' logo painted on the bottom of their Boeing 737 fleet. Their customer service focus is legendary. And Southwest communicates it constantly, virtually everywhere—even in the restrooms.

"Vision" is not just customer experience. There needs to be an expectation regarding profitability, growth, quality, and employee retention. The maverick leader's Vision, therefore, should encompass all of these items, and can be both quantitative and qualitative when defining a company's Culture and associated Vision.

'Safe Harbors' & Served Markets

Served Markets include products, target borrowers, geographical market selection, and channel selection. Since the financial crisis, very little product outside of conventional, government, and jumbo fixed rate has been offered. Hybrid 5/1, 7/1, and 10/1 adjustable rate mortgages have been offered, but constitute a small segment of the market. The private label securitization market is just beginning to show increased activity. The non-QM market has not evolved to any material extent.

In 2010, I attended a meeting with Richard Cordray, Director of the Consumer Financial Protection Bureau, and a number of mortgage bankers at a session arranged by Dave Stevens, CEO of the Mortgage Bankers Association of America. The topic at hand was proposed Qualified Mortgage regulations and the then lack of "safe harbor"[62] provisions. During the meeting, a Cordray deputy

---

[62] 'Safe Harbor' provides substantially reduced potential litigation risk for loans that fall into the 'safe harbor' provisions of Qualified Mortgage Lending.

stated that lenders didn't need a safe harbor. The mortgage bankers pushed back, stating that regulatory certainty and bright lines regarding supervision and enforcement were very important. Mr. Cordray asked for a show of hands of lenders that thought safe harbor was not necessary for QM lending. No hands went up. Given the reputation risks and punitive enforcements that were underway, the lenders felt the need for the protection from litigation and enforcement that a safe harbor provision would supply. Mr. Cordray[63] appeared skeptical, but progress was made to create a "safe harbor" for QM lending.

If it was necessary to fight for a Qualified Mortgage lending safe harbor, lenders intuitively knew non-QM lending would be slow to come. Certainly, reputation risk combined with regulation has kept products to primarily fixed rate and hybrid products, with industry caution preventing product development much beyond the Qualified Mortgage box.

The "Qualified Mortgage" provides a "safe harbor" against private rights of action by borrowers. This apparent legal protection may be considered as protecting banks and investors in mortgages against frivolous litigation. But safe harbor has a perverse impact. It has a major dampening effect on product innovation. As Patrick Sinks commented on the "shell shock" in the boardroom over litigation, there are few executives that would seek to innovate when the question from compliance or a board member might sound like this: "Let me get this straight: you want to forego safe harbor, expose us to litigation and make loans that are out of the box. Why?" So much for innovation in all but the most confident board rooms.

---

[63] Recently Mr. Cordray announced his resignation from the CFPB in November 2017.

Qualified Mortgage and Ability to Repay

Perhaps the biggest opportunity in mortgage product innovation lies in expanding credit access to non-traditional borrowers. Credit scoring models may exclude applicants that do not fit the traditional FICO scoring model. A competitive product suggests it can score several million qualified applicants that are excluded by the traditional FICO model, but the GSEs have not moved to adopt such a model.

Computation and documentation of income from borrowers working in the so-called "gig" economy, millennials with a high level of student debt, immigrants that work in family-owned businesses, employees and contractors paid mostly in cash, and employees with frequent job changes or multiple part-time jobs all present challenges to traditional mortgage banking processes.

The cost of housing in certain geographies also presents some mortgage banking challenges, causing high loan-to-value and high debt-to-income ratios and difficulties at qualification under the 'ATR' regulations. Slim inventories of homes for sale put upward pressure on both housing prices and monthly rents. The multi-million-dollar price of entry-level housing in some markets excludes a large segment of the population that could buy a home in a less expensive geography. High rents make it challenging for families seeking shelter to have a viable alternative to buying a home.

Customer Experience as a Transformational Strategy

Customer experience is how a lender builds the confidence and trust of the borrower. Customer experience varies by consumer channel selection and consumer preference, as well as consumer demographics. It's critically important to factor in the other non-mortgage experiences a customer may have when considering the customer's experience in buying a mortgage.

AMAZON'S BUSINESS MODEL CANVAS				
KEY PARTNERS	KEY ACTIVITIES	VALUE PROPOSITION	CUSTOMER RELATIONSHIP	CUSTOMER SEGMENT
Logistics Partner	Merchandising	Convenience	Self-Service	Individual Leverage
Affiliates	Production and Design	Price	Automated Services	Group Leverage
Authors and Publishers	KEY RESOURCES	Instant Fulfillment with eReader	DISTRIBUTION CHANNELS	Global Consumer Market
Network of Sellers	Physical Warehouses	Vast Selection	Affiliates	
	Human, Web Application & Development		Application Interfaces	
			Amazon.com	
			Sale of Assets	
% COST STRUCTURE		REVENUE STREAMS		
Low Cost Structure		E-books and Content		
IT and Fulfillment Infrastructure		Acquisitions and Investments		
Economies of Scale		Commission on Reseller Sales		

In the online world, the Amazon experience sets the standard. The Amazon experience is tightly integrated, from the customer's first point of contact right through to ease of shipping. Then consider the lending process model on the following chart, introduced at the beginning of this book. Which model is clearer? Which one would a consumer prefer? Enough said.

Some lenders, too, need to consider how to define the third-party originator ("TPO") experience (if the lender serves this channel). How will the lender serve technically able TPOs? How about less technically able TPOs, especially smaller mortgage brokers? How will document management be accomplished? Exception management?

A clear definition of customer experience, by channel, will lead to process and workflow decisions. One doesn't fly on an airplane without having issues such as destination, travel purpose, travel class, travel objectives, travel budget, and timing in mind. Like trip planning, the lending destination definition should include quantitative metrics such as customer satisfaction, service level times, profitability, defect-free loan files, as well as qualitative factors such as a pleasing customer experience, fast closing, and establishing a good customer relationship.

Optimizing Process and Workflow

The mortgage banking process is very complicated and highly regulated. The process used by a lender describes what has to be accomplished to move from the very beginning of the customer's interest in your company, all the way through taking the application, closing the loan, establishing the loan servicing experience, and serving that customer's financing needs for life. All of this, too, must happen in a manner that meets a customer's expectations.

Workflow is how the lender's process is translated into the individual tasks necessary to complete the loan. Workflow extends all the way down to the smallest factors within each task within the process. Many lender workflows appear to have a large amount of variability when it comes to the "what" and "how" of accomplishing each task. Most loan origination systems support milestones as a form of workflow management, but the tasks within each milestone are generally not planned and executed as they would be in a typical manufacturing operation.

This lack of planning and execution can result in a large variance when it comes to how, when, and how long it takes to execute each task. If a loan processor has been processing for twenty years, the processor pretty much knows what to do and when to do it. If a processor is new to mortgage banking, the how, what, and when of doing things can be a trial and error process. We have studied various loan officer/loan processor/underwriter/closer combinations. Some combinations are remarkably effective. These remarkably effective combinations result when expectations for each and every party are clear, agreed to by all, and followed consistently. Given these requirements, it's not surprising that most combinations are not remarkably effective.

Time and again workflow is not well known and agreed to by all parties. This strikes me as unusual, since workflow is a key element to the desired customer experience. Why leave that to chance? How does a lender claim to "manufacture" loans when the lending workflow has not been reduced to a standard set of tasks, service levels, and monitoring protocols? If your workflow cannot be documented and standardized, you are leaving much to chance and, what's more, leaving much to the individual decisions of employees... including some employees that may be very new and inexperienced.

Workflow seems most difficult in traditional retail environments. The individuality of the branch manager and loan officer often put pressure on adapting the branch's view of how the process and workflow should function. If a lender allows diversity in branch practice, the corresponding control has to be definitive and non-negotiable service levels at both the borrower and support team level. One cannot run an efficient and compliant process if the branch demands diversity and practice but refuses to be held accountable to service levels – both internal and external.

Future Technology

Bitcoin keeps making the news. Bitcoin is a secure, anonymized store of value. Bitcoin uses a technology called Blockchain as an element of the technical platform that enables Bitcoin. Blockchain is a shared unchangeable ledger for recording the history of transactions. In mortgage banking, transactions logged via Blockchain could include the receipt of trusted borrower information, such as bank account data, income data, and related qualifying information. The data comes from a trusted source (such as a bank, IRS, or payroll service) and never needs to be re-verified. The source data for a borrower mortgage file could all be available from independent trusted sources. No more copies of bank statements, W-2, etc.

The consumer's record could also be appended in real time. Meaning once the basic customer information at loan inception is created, the ongoing transactional history could be built in real time. The transaction history (upon consent of the customer) could be continued past closing and through the entire servicing life of the loan. One may say, "We can do that now with credit reports." True, but what could be very valuable is the combination of real-time, up-to-date banking, income, tax and payment history all in one place. Combine it with information on the homeowner's collateral value and comparable transaction records and imagine having an authenticated complete history of a consumer's finances available for an instant credit decision since all of the information has been assembled from trusted parties! No checkers checking the checkers. No robotics. Just authentic real-time data.

This blockchain record of authenticated up-to-the-minute data could change the landscape of loan origination. This means the party owning the servicing could essentially offer a refinance or additional credit or wealth management services, if the consumer grants permission. Servicing could finally reach its highest value not as a series of cash flows but as a relationship bond with the customer.

Dave Stevens of the MBA believes there is a need for a "Bright Line" between primary originations and secondary market agencies. The GSEs will likely be one of the sponsors of authenticated data, and the step from buying loans to making loans could be a very small step indeed.

Uniform data sets required by the GSEs provide data standard-ization and uniformity, as well as the ability for GSEs to acquire borrower data from trusted independent sources. The GSEs offer lenders representation and warranty relief on key data components plus more speed and simplicity. Lenders may receive partial relief from representations and warranties on the appraised value for eli-gible properties that pass collateral evaluation tools from the GSEs.

As Andrew Bon Salle of Fannie Mae states, "Electronic validation of income, assets, and employment lets lenders and borrowers benefit by moving away from the manual processes prevalent in the indus-try today."[64] Fannie Mae in particular sees the potential in creating a comprehensive and ongoing data repository of an extended dataset regarding mortgage customers. Both GSEs have monthly feeds on borrower payment performance, and both are working on building an extensive database regarding collateral values and local market conditions among other things. Perhaps one or both of the GSEs will emerge as a host of a Blockchain enabled repository of data.

This could be very healthy for the industry, given that the majority of loans flowing through the GSEs or their AUS engines. It will require prompt action on the "Bright Line" to ensure GSEs stay on their sec-ondary market role and steer clear of the primary origination market.

Technology

So, when asking lender CEOs how satisfied they are with their tech-nology (CRM and lead management, loan origination system, pric-ing engine, secondary marketing systems, servicing system, among

[64] http://www.fanniemae.com/portal/research-insights/perspectives/day-1-certainty-bon-salle-030217.html

others), the answers ran from pretty satisfied to not satisfied at all. The answers I received from lenders parallel survey results from Stratmor and other market participants.

But in considering technology, one must think about the rapid evolution of trusted, independent, first-generation data available regarding bank accounts, employment and earnings, IRS data etc. This data is available from FormFree, Avantus, CoreLogic, DataVerify, Equifax, (including The Work Number®), Finicity, First American Mortgage Solutions, PointServ, Taxdoor, Veri-Tax, among others. When thinking about the future of mortgage banking and how to speed the process and reduce the cost of origination, one must consider how direct access to trusted data can change the mortgage banking landscape for various lenders.

I have noted a correlation between satisfaction with technology and coherence of vision, culture, desired customer experience, process, and workflow. Lenders with well-defined vision, culture and desired customer experience, process and workflow are generally much happier with their technology systems than those lenders that have not linked each of these elements of the value chain. Technology providers confide that the better defined and documented the elements discussed above are, the better able the lender is to obtain results from the technology.

The CEOs of some of the most successful and technologically satisfied lenders stated that their teams designed the process from the *back end* (Servicing in the case of many lenders) moving forward to customer contact. Steven Covey explained the basis of this approach in his *Seven Habits of Highly Effective People*[65]: His second habit is "Begin with the End in Mind". According to Covey, this habit "is

---

[65] Steven R. Covey, Seven Habits of Highly Effective People, Chapter 2, Franklin Covey Co., 1990.

based on imagination—the ability to envision in your mind what you cannot at present see with your eyes. It is based on the principle that all things are created twice. There is a mental (first) creation, and a physical (second) creation. The physical creation follows the mental, just as a building follows a blueprint. If you don't make a conscious effort to visualize who you are and what you want in life, then you empower other people and circumstances to shape you and your life by default."

Defining the back-end or destination helps shape the overall process as a conscious choice, not as something that is left to circumstances. Customer satisfaction, service level timeframes, defect-free loan file. No rework or investor stipulations prior to secondary market sale and superior profitability are all influenced by the process. It's much more difficult to correct an error or exception downstream as opposed to correcting it early in the process. If one designs from the backend forward, it forces each process and workflow to be standardized and optimized to deliver the desired result.

This means employees aren't trying to fix issues in post-closing that should have been detected and corrected much earlier in the process. In speaking with one CEO, he mentioned that he found that the difficulty and cost of correcting an error increased significantly the more milestones that were passed between the error and its detection and correction. An example: one lender had a systemic issue in determining the need for flood insurance. When detected by the correspondent lender, prior to funding the loan to be purchased from the mortgage banker, the dislocation and customer service nightmares were orders of magnitude higher than if the flood determination and follow-through would have occurred very early in the loan process. This was a basic systemic error and could have been easily prevented, yet the frequency with which we see this error suggests that often little thought is given to the back-end destination of loan files with no errors within the file.

A reader might say, "That's not happening in my company." Well, take a look at prefunding QC reports, post-close exception reports, correspondent funding stipulations, trailing document defects, post-closing quality assurance, investor delivery exceptions, internal audits, compliance findings, etc. Few exceptions? That's the evidence of a well-defined and coherent process. Many exceptions? Maybe one needs to consider a re-think of the process starting at the back-end forward.

I once showed my loan exception lists to a CEO of a high-quality manufacturer of industrial products. He was shocked to see so many exceptions compared to the number of loans. He was thinking a few defects per thousand loans, not multiple defects per loan. His conclusion: poor definition of customer experience, process, and workflow.

My bruised ego recovered, and I worked hard on better definitions of expectations, process, workflow, service levels, and defect rates. The concentration on these elements served us really well, boosting profitability and customer satisfaction, and lowering risk of repurchase. We focused on earning high customer satisfaction, 100 basis points or more of pre-tax profit, low cost and high employee retention metrics.

Another way to think about process and workflow is to consider a similar industry that is highly regulated, consumer-facing, and with a high volume of transactions. One such industry is the airline industry. I thought about comments by Southwest Airlines CEO Gary Kelly, paraphrased here: "We must get the thousands of mechanical parts in a 737 to work in concert with pilots, ground personnel, air traffic control and others. There must be perfect execution." Southwest consistently lands a 200,000-pound aircraft moving about 130 miles per hour at touchdown in all types of weather with up to 180 people on board, over a thousand times a day. Southwest uses only one aircraft type (Boeing 737-xxx) in its fleet so all pilots and mechanics are certified to fly and maintain all aircraft.

Airline transport procedures begins each flight with the end in mind. What is the weather forecast at the destination airport? Alternate airports in case the destination is unavailable for any reason. Fuel needed? Special requirements of passengers and special cargo? The list goes on with weight and aircraft balance computations, wind speeds at various altitudes, etc.

The process of actually flying a 737 after flight planning is rigorously documented, and pilots train regularly to demonstrate proficiency. The process is so well defined that any Southwest pilot can fly every Southwest aircraft. The pilot's responsibilities and process flow are well documented through all phases of aircraft operation.

The following is a Boeing 737 checklist, from start-up to shut down. Note that the process is the same for every flight. The workflow proceeds smoothly from start to finish, and documentation exists for each underlying task within the workflow. Note that emergency situations such as cabin pressurization loss, engine fire, or engine loss resulting in drift down are all covered, as well as the mundane workflow items such as when to turn on the seatbelt sign. The checklist covers key aspects of every phase of flight but does not replace pilot experience and judgement in unusual situations. The whole checklist[66] from the pilot first boarding the plance to last engine shutdown of the day is below:

The "before landing" subsection is reproduced in more readable form below. Ever key action is outlined, from configuring the "Engine Start" switches to "Cont" (continuous ignition in case of unexpected engine ingestion of heavy precipitation for an instant restart) to how to configure the AP (autopilot) and AT (auto throttles) for various instrument approaches, including Category III Autoland in zero visibility with zero ceiling. The point is that every situation is considered, and the appropriate configuration is documented.

---

[66] Example 737 Checklist by Ian Mancz

As a lender, are the different issues that may arise in a loan documented for each member of your team, for each position? Would that help employees, especially new employees or employees with limited tenure in the industry?

In the airlines, all of this happens this way for very important reasons, which shouldn't surprise anyone. Deviation from standard procedures can have bad results. According to the National Safety Transportation Board crash investigation report[67]:

"On July 22, 2013 Southwest Airlines flight 345, landed hard, nose-first, on runway 4 at New York's LaGuardia Airport. Of the 144 passengers and five crewmembers on board, eight sustained minor injuries and the airplane was substantially damaged.

Contributing to the accident was the captain's failure to comply with standard operating procedures during the approach. National Transportation Safety Board [found that the first officer was conducting the approach, and the captain took control away from the first officer, but not until the plane was 27 feet above the ground. This late transfer of control from the first officer to the captain resulted in neither pilot being able to effectively monitor the airplane's altitude and pitch attitude. According to the Southwest Airlines Flight Operations Manual, the captain should have called for a go-around well before this point in the approach instead of trying to salvage the landing.

For example, Southwest's stabilized approach criteria require an immediate go-around if the airplane flaps are not in the final landing configuration by 1,000 feet above the ground. In this case, the flaps were not correctly set until the airplane was 500 feet above the ground.

The National Transportation Safety Board determines the probable cause(s) of this accident were the captain's attempt

---

[67] https://www.ntsb.gov/_layouts/ntsb.aviation/brief.aspx?ev_id=20130723X13256&key=1

to recover from an unstabilized approach by transferring airplane control at low altitude instead of performing a go-around. Contributing to the accident was the captain's failure to comply with standard operating procedures.

The crash of Southwest flight 345 was a tragic result of multiple failures to follow established safety procedures. The crash is instructive in that the captain was experienced, and the aircraft was equipped with the latest technology. The captain committed very serious operational procedure deviations. Yet over 8,000 flights occur daily in the U.S., all ending with a safe landing. The process works… except when blatantly ignored.

Making loans does not have the safety consequences of flying an aircraft, and no parallel in this regard should be drawn. But, the need for standardized process and workflow in the lending process are still required. There are economic consequences for a failure to follow standardized process and workflow. Deviations can carry significant economic, legal and regulatory consequences. It is not advisable to have a very loose lending process where much is left to the individual skills of the loan production and operational staff.

Results

At the end of the day, the measurable outputs of a well-defined process, workflow, and technology plan are customer satisfaction, profitability, cost, loan defects, and employee retention. Don't worry about best practice, worry about what produces acceptable outputs in your company. A few examples:

- One lender CEO produced outstanding results with a traditional retail focus on FHA/VA loans, with a very pronounced effort for loans to be closed on time. His team catered to realtors that needed purchase business, particularly Federal Housing Administration ("FHA"), and closed quickly and "without drama". The reward was profitability of four times the MBA average pretax profit—*consistently.* He stayed focused to that strategy, and measured the appropriate items, set rigid service level standards and expected his team to deliver. This lender used "out of the box" technology set up for his process. The lender's vision was simply getting the borrower "home on time". A straightforward promise, executed exceedingly well and with a clear strategic vision.

- Another CEO lender produced outstanding customer service quality, attaining the number one position in a national survey for multiple years in a row by using a pure direct to consumer strategy, using self-designed software, and earning outstanding financial returns.

- Poor results are likely when ignoring a well-defined process and workflow. The CEO of one bank-owned mortgage bank literally catered to branch managers, allowing the branch managers to dictate many operational aspects of the lending process. She paid them far beyond fair compensation. Poor processes, poor controls, and excessive compensation cause the bank economic losses, as well as reputational risks. This CEO appeared to have little regard for process, workflow, or structure. The bank endured substantial economic damage, reputational damage, poor customer service, high costs, and high turnover, all resulting from a very public issue regarding fair lending matters and regulatory and business process matters in general.

The longer I am in the mortgage banking business, the more I am convinced that the elements of success—vision, culture, customer experience, process, workflow, technology and expected results— are directly linked. The successful CEOs interviewed for this book confirmed that sentiment. Keep this model (pictured below) in mind as you work through the book.

Remember that "Results" (outputs) can be whatever one defines. For this book, "Results" are measured in data-driven customer satisfaction, superior profitability, cost, and employee retention, among other things. If you take one thing from this Executive Summary, it is to specify and measure data-driven output and results expected, measure them frequently, and hold your team accountable to produce the results you require.

Made in the USA
Las Vegas, NV
19 January 2022

41842076R00154